PAUL
ROBESON

Also by Martin Duberman

NONFICTION

*Naomi Weisstein: Brain Scientist, Rock Band
Leader, Feminist Rebel (Her Collected Essays)*

Has the Gay Movement Failed?

*The Rest of It: Hustlers, Cocaine, Depression,
and Then Some, 1976–1988*

*The Emperor Has No Clothes: Doug
Ireland's Radical Voice* (editor)

The Martin Duberman Reader

*Hold Tight Gently: Michael Callen, Essex
Hemphill, and the Battlefield of AIDS*

Howard Zinn: A Life on the Left

*A Saving Remnant: The Radical Lives of
Barbara Deming and David McReynolds*

Waiting to Land: A (Mostly) Political Memoir

The Worlds of Lincoln Kirstein

Left Out: The Politics of Exclusion: Essays, 1964–2002

Queer Representations (editor)

A Queer World (editor)

Midlife Queer: Autobiography of a Decade, 1971–1981

Stonewall

Cures: A Gay Man's Odyssey

*Hidden from History: Reclaiming the Gay
and Lesbian Past* (co-editor)

Paul Robeson: A Biography
About Time: Exploring the Gay Past
Black Mountain: An Exploration in Community
The Uncompleted Past
James Russell Lowell
The Antislavery Vanguard (editor)
Charles Francis Adams, 1807–1886
Andrea Dworkin: The Feminist as Revolutionary

DRAMA
Radical Acts
Male Armor: Selected Plays, 1968–1974
The Memory Bank

FICTION
Luminous Traitor
Jews/Queers/Germans
Haymarket

YOUNG ADULT
Lives of Notable Gay Men and Lesbians (10 volumes, editor)
Issues in Lesbian and Gay Life (4 volumes, editor)

PAUL ROBESON

NO ONE CAN SILENCE ME

Adapted for Young Adults

MARTIN DUBERMAN

Foreword by Jason Reynolds

THE NEW PRESS

NEW YORK
LONDON

Requests for permission to reproduce selections from this book should be made through our website: https://thenewpress.com/contact.

Published in the United States by The New Press, New York, 2021
Distributed by Two Rivers Distribution

ISBN 978-1-62079-649-4 (hc)
ISBN 978-1-62097-661-6 (ebook)
CIP data is available

The New Press publishes books that promote and enrich public discussion and understanding of the issues vital to our democracy and to a more equitable world. These books are made possible by the enthusiasm of our readers; the support of a committed group of donors, large and small; the collaboration of our many partners in the independent media and the not-for-profit sector; booksellers, who often hand-sell New Press books; librarians; and above all by our authors.

www.thenewpress.com

Composition by Dix!
This book was set in Fairfield Light

Printed in the United States of America

10 9 8 7 6 5 4 3 2 1

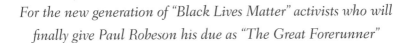

*For the new generation of "Black Lives Matter" activists who will
finally give Paul Robeson his due as "The Great Forerunner"*

As an artist I come to sing, but as a citizen, I will always speak for peace, and no one can silence me in this.

—Paul Robeson

Contents

Foreword

JASON REYNOLDS

ON A SATURDAY MORNING IN 1988—MAYBE 1989—WITH Rice Krispies and sugar milk still on my breath, I sat on the side of my parents' bed. It had become tradition for my father and me to watch old movies, usually dusty cowboy flicks or goofy comedies where a slap on the head sounds like a bicycle horn. But on this day, there was something else, someone else, on the screen. A man towering over his co-stars, his body a little thicker, his hair a little thicker, his voice a little thicker. I remember his baritone sounding so strange to me, an alien timbre, because up until that moment I'd assumed my father had the deepest voice in the world. But this man on the television's voice was deeper. Much deeper.

"Who is that?" I asked my father.

"That," he said with a flicker of pride in his eyes, "is Paul Robeson."

I'd heard that lilt in my father's voice a few times before then. That bell in his throat always seemed to ring at the mention of men he admired. Muhammad Ali. Dr. King. Michael Jordan. Stevie Wonder. His own father—my grandfather—a blind man named Brooke. And in this moment I knew to put Robeson on that list. But my father never said why. Didn't give me any of his usual adventure tales about how he'd met Robeson at a grimy diner somewhere or how he thought we might be related to him, because according to my father we were related to everyone. Instead, he just said Paul Robeson's name, then turned back to the black and white moving across the screen.

The truth is, I didn't get it then. The film itself didn't strike me, especially since I was used to Saturday morning movies involving small-town sheriffs or slapstick shenanigans. And I never had a chance to revisit the conversation because a few years later, my family changed. There were no more Saturday morning movies. No more sitting on the side of the bed, because my father slept in a different one, in a different house, and our relationship had become the Wild West, dry and overheated with no room for questions. But fortunately, years later when I got to college Robeson's name was invoked, this time by a professor. And just like with my father, the professor who brought Robeson up seemed to have light sitting on the back of his tongue. All I knew was that name and that voice. But this teacher would unfold this man's story, and the myth of the bottom-voiced giant would make the rest of us, including bored-to-death seventeen-year-olds like me, feel like . . . more. Like the mere acknowledgment of his life could, and did, cast a spell on the uninspired, which is why it was such a shame I hadn't heard anything about this man since I was six. Since my father. Nothing in middle school. Not a word in high school.

This book, *Paul Robeson: No One Can Silence Me*, will fix that, will make sure your more-ness is made plain, now.

Here you will learn:
About a Black man whose father was a slave.

About a Black man who, despite that, was a superstar college athlete as well as valedictorian.

About a Black man who then becomes a lawyer.

About a Black man who, after facing racism in the legal profession, becomes an actor and singer.

About a Black man who sang in several languages and lived abroad.

About a Black man who arguably became the most famous Black man in the world.

And, with all the notoriety and success, understood he was still a Black man, and fought for the freedom of his people.

Here's what you will *really* learn:

You. Maybe a you you have yet to meet. And maybe this will be the introduction of you, today, to future-you. Because though Paul Robeson's story is impressive (you'll see!) and explains why his name seems to lift off the tongues of all who say it, what his life really serves as is perhaps the greatest reminder of the possibilities of a single person. That's right. This is a story about you. About me. About our potential to be whole, to be stocked with interest and ideas. To be fully free in the parts of ourselves we can control, and to fight for freedom against the parts of our society that have convinced us that we are to be controlled. That we could be all that we are, limitlessly. That sitting on the side of the bed watching cops and clowns is a comfortable tradition, but one that at some point has to end. If not, we may never know what Paul Robeson knew—what you are about to find out—that there is a world within us, but there is no world without us.

Introduction

PERFORMANCE
AND PROTEST

IN FEBRUARY 1942, ONE OF AMERICA'S BEST-KNOWN
singers and actors stepped onto a stage in Kansas City, Missouri. Robeson's eyes scanned the auditorium as he performed the first half of his concert. Both white and Black people had gathered to hear him—not unusual for one of the foremost Black artists of his time. But Robeson saw that the Black concertgoers had been seated in the top balcony—the worst seats and the farthest from the stage.

When the program reached its intermission, Robeson left the stage, applause ringing in his ears. When he returned, he startled the audience by announcing that he'd complete the second half of his program—but only under protest.

"I have made a lifelong habit," he told the crowd, "of refusing to sing in southern states or anywhere that audiences are segregated"; he had agreed to perform the concert, he added, only after having been assured that there would be no separation by race in the auditorium. Though Robeson finished the second half, he made a point of including in it a passionate rendition of the antisegregation ballad "Jim Crow." And he sang it, as a local critic later wrote, "with stronger feeling than he had put into any other number." Several white audience members got the message and left in the middle of the song. By the end of the concert, a hundred more had followed them out.

The very next day, Robeson learned that his hotel reservation in Santa Fe, New Mexico, where he was scheduled to sing, had been canceled. The head of the concert series tried to justify the cancellation by saying that New Mexico was close to "the southern states," where opposition to racial equality was widespread. Robeson promptly refused to fulfill the Santa Fe concert date.

National newspapers reported both the Kansas City and Santa Fe incidents. And an editor of the *Call*, a Black newspaper in Kansas City, wrote to thank Robeson "for the stand you took against segregation in our Municipal Auditorium here." She called Robeson's act "a good start" and hoped it would inspire the city's Black residents to protest race-based separation in tax-supported buildings.

Performance and protest were mingled throughout Paul Robeson's life. He was an extraordinary artist of strong principles who harbored a deep belief that the world could become a better, fairer place—and who paid a high personal price for holding fast to his ideals. In this regard he was a forerunner of other gifted, famous Americans of color. One of them was boxing champion Muhammad Ali, who was stripped of his titles in 1966 after his religious beliefs and opposition to the Vietnam War led him to refuse to be drafted into the military. Two years later, runners Tommie Smith and John Carlos were booed after raising their fists—a gesture that has been called both a

Paul Robeson's 1917–1918 Rutgers yearbook photograph

Black Power salute and a human rights salute—as they stood on the winners' podium of the Mexico City Olympic Games while "The Star-Spangled Banner" played.

Closer to the present, quarterback Colin Kaepernick was shunned by the National Football League after kneeling during the national anthem in 2016 to protest racial injustice and police brutality. That same year, the entire Indiana Fever team of the Women's National Basketball Association also took a knee in protest, and three WNBA teams were fined for wearing Black Lives Matter T-shirts. As the BLM movement grew, Black WNBA players such as Natasha Cloud and Renee Montgomery stepped away from their professional careers for whole seasons to work for justice and reform.

As both a legendary performer and an early champion of Black rights, Paul Robeson stands tall in the history of American arts *and* in the history of the nation's—and the world's—struggle for equality. As a performer he achieved enormous acclaim, only to fall from grace when his conscience clashed with the politics of his time. Today, amid calls for social change and a reckoning with racism, Robeson's unwavering insistence on the dignity of all people is as powerful and inspiring as ever.

When Paul Robeson, whose father had been enslaved, graduated from Rutgers University at the top of his class in 1919, it was widely predicted that he would become "the leader of the colored race in America." His magnetic personality and his sweeping range of abilities and gifts made that prediction seem entirely likely. His achievements in the two decades after graduation confirmed it.

Following graduation from Columbia University with a law degree, Robeson became an internationally renowned star of stage and screen, as well as a singer who regularly sold out concert halls as the foremost interpreter of Black spirituals and work songs.

By 1940 Robeson had become esteemed among many white and almost all Black people—although for different reasons. Black Americans saw in him proof that, when given the opportunity, they could reach the highest rungs of the ladder of achievement. White Americans praised him as proof that "the system" worked: that anyone could rise to the top through hard work and determination—together with the right attitude, which meant a lack of disrespect or combativeness.

Those who knew Robeson personally were well aware that, even early on, he was far more complicated than his public image

Paul Robeson in the first-year class at Columbia Law School, 1920

as a "striver" who played by the rules. They knew that throughout the 1930s he'd increasingly immersed himself in the study of Africa, and that he'd become a passionate critic of racism and an outspoken champion of oppressed peoples everywhere.

Those convictions never changed. In fact, over time, they deepened, as Robeson came to see that his own fame and success did not reflect the lesser opportunities open to most people. Up to the end of World War II in 1945, it was still possible for him to believe that democracy would spread at home after the defeat of fascism abroad: racial barriers in the United States would disappear, and the colonized countries in Africa and Asia would be freed from the yoke of imperialism.

Yet if Robeson's progressive views remained constant over the years, the political landscape shifted dramatically after the war. In the United States especially, the climate of opinion swerved to the right, culminating in the 1950s with the rise of "McCarthyism," a government-sponsored witch hunt designed to punish dissenters of all kinds.

Throughout Robeson remained steadfast, refusing to abandon his principles. The country's failure to make good on its promises of democracy brought out in him not submission but uncompromising anger. His refusal to submit brought down on his head the zealous wrath of the conservative right—*and* the FBI. Branded a communist and a traitor, he had his passport lifted, preventing him from the travel that had been a vital part of his life. His concert and acting offers dried up, and under constant stress and surveillance, his health deteriorated.

Within a single decade, Robeson's image shifted from public hero to public enemy. He became an outcast, cut off from opportunities and audiences alike, who spent the last decade of his life living in a room in his sister's house in Philadelphia.

This extraordinary turnabout in one of the great American success stories was not simply a tragedy for Robeson himself. It was a marker in the decline of American leadership in the international struggle for a fairer, more just world—a struggle that continues to this day.

This book tells Paul Robeson's story.

PAUL
ROBESON

Chapter 1

A BOY'S BALANCING ACT

PAUL ROBESON WAS BORN IN THE TOWN OF PRINCE-ton, New Jersey, on April 9, 1898. Of the seven children born into his family, only five lived past infancy. Paul was the youngest. At the time of his birth, his father was fifty-three years old and his mother forty-five.

Paul's father, the Reverend William Drew Robeson, had been born in slavery in Martin County, North Carolina. After escaping to freedom in Pennsylvania at the age of fifteen, he'd managed to get an education and to become a minister. Paul's mother, Maria Louisa Bustill Robeson, was a teacher. She traced her roots back to the Bantu people of Africa, and members of her family had long been prominent in such antislavery organizations as the Free African Society and the Underground Railroad.

Childhood Challenges

Slavery had ended decades before Paul was born, but like much of the country, Princeton strictly followed the rules of what was called "Jim Crow": a set of laws and customs that made Black people second-class citizens. They were kept out of "Whites

Who Was Jim Crow?

Was Jim Crow a real person? Probably not, but in the 1830s, white audiences laughed at a stage character of that name played by a white actor named Thomas Dartmouth Rice, who darkened his face and hands to perform in so-called minstrel shows. These shows—performed by Black people as well as by white people in blackface—were based on stereotypes and caricatures of African Americans as dim-witted and clumsy. Rice's minstrel show became so popular in the United States and Great Britain that people started using "Jim Crow" as an insulting name for any Black person.

Minstrel shows faded in popularity, but the term "Jim Crow" made a comeback in the late nineteenth and early twentieth centuries. After the North won the Civil War and slavery was ended, the Southern states struck back by passing laws that limited Black rights and freedoms. These so-called Jim Crow laws created a system of legalized racial discrimination in the South. In the North, Black people were discriminated against in other ways, including banks refusing to lend them money and employers refusing to hire them. Today "Jim Crow" or "the Jim Crow era" refers to the period when the law enforced racial discrimination in some states, while custom upheld it in others.

Only" spaces such as train cars, restaurants, and movie theaters and forced to use separate and inferior facilities. Although Black Americans were citizens, a complex network of regulations kept most of them from taking part in public life through voting or holding office.

Princeton's Black community had grown after the American Revolution, when formerly enslaved people who had fought in the war won their freedom and settled in the area. That community grew larger during the nineteenth century, and by the time of Paul Robeson's birth, it included Black businesses and churches. The great majority of the town's Black adults, though, were held to menial jobs, and their children went to a Black-only school that ran only through the eighth grade.

The white citizens of Princeton shared the view that was dominant in the country at that time: that Black people were inferior beings. White Princetonians read such books as *The Negro a Beast* (1900) or *The Negro: A Menace to Civilization* (1907). A few years later, they flocked to see D.W. Griffith's 1915 movie *The Birth of a Nation*, which applauded those who took the law into their own hands in order to punish Black people who'd stepped out of line. Between 1900 and 1914, eleven hundred people of color were lynched or burned to death in the United States. In 1912 President Woodrow Wilson extended segregation, or separation by race, to all federal office buildings, and he automatically rejected Black applicants for jobs in government services.

When the Reverend Robeson spoke out vigorously against racial discrimination, he was forced from his pulpit after twenty years of service. He had to piece together an income by doing odd jobs, including hauling ashes for the townspeople and working as a coachman carting Princeton University students around town. More devastating still was the death of his wife when a coal from their stove fell on her long skirt. Badly burned, she died after lingering for days in enormous pain.

Paul was six years old when he lost what he later called his

*The Rex Theatre for Colored People in LeLand,
Mississippi—an example of Jim Crow segregation*

"sweet, generous-hearted" mother. Only he and one brother still lived at home, with grief and economic hardship their daily companions. Yet the Reverend Robeson refused to give in to despair or bitterness. He "was made of flintstone," his son Paul later said; though he witnessed his father "taunted by the hideous injustices of the color 'bar,'" he never once saw in the man even "a hint of servility."

Held to High Standards

As a father, Reverend Robeson was loving but demanding, a strict disciplinarian with perfectionist standards. He cared deeply for his son but rarely indulged him. Paul was expected all at once to shoulder family chores, work at odd jobs to help pay for school fees, and achieve top ranking as a student. At twelve he worked as a kitchen boy; at fourteen he toiled part-time as a farm worker; at sixteen he held down a man's job in brickyards and shipyards; and in his late teens he spent summers working as a waiter at a small hotel in Rhode Island.

In all these activities Paul strove to meet his father's high standards—and succeeded. He became an efficient, reliable worker, a promising athlete, and an outstanding scholar. Because the only school he could attend in Princeton ended with the eighth grade, he commuted to the nearby town of Somerville for high school. There it was discovered that he had a remarkable singing voice. Paul's mostly white classmates might ordinarily have resented such a gifted paragon. Instead, his laidback nature and modesty won him many admirers, though social mingling was frowned upon.

The Reverend Robeson had taught his son well. He'd instilled in Paul the necessity of self-discipline, and the importance for a Black boy of never boasting about his accomplishments and remaining unfailingly "nice" when praised for them. He must always know his "place" and "act right." He must be polite and friendly at all times, never arrogant. Even when he turned in a superb performance, he had to pretend it was merely average. This was especially important, his father taught him, in the presence of white people, given their assumption of superiority.

The adult Robeson would later write that his father drummed into his head the need "to do nothing to give them cause to fear you, for then the oppressing hand, which might at times ease up a little, will surely become a fist to knock you down again!"

Paul developed the ability to size up a person immediately—though he learned to keep his insights to himself. Yet there was a downside to keeping himself under tight control. It became second nature for Paul to conceal his deepest feelings, to remain apart, to become something of a loner. No one with Robeson's extraordinary talents could constantly minimize them in public, presenting himself as ordinary, without the deception taking a toll—especially since it conflicted with his father's other message: to be true to himself. There was another concern as well. During a time of profound racism, Paul knew that he'd had what he later called a relatively easy time of it "in comparison to most Negroes." To complain might make him appear ungrateful, even to his fellow Black Americans.

Yet Robeson was human, and under unusual pressure his self-control could crack. Later in life he wrote, "I get a little mad, man, get a little angry, and when I get angry I can be awful rough." As a young man, though, not yet burdened with too much anger, he was still able to juggle his father's double instruction to be proud *and* pleasant.

Like anyone who grows up Black in America, Paul experienced his share of racial abuse, but it hadn't become the reigning fact of his life. And his father had also taught him that not every white person was racist and that he should judge people as individuals, rather than automatically assuming that all white people were bigoted. But in later years, when Paul became persecuted for his political views, his anger and secretiveness would deepen. One close friend said, "Paul had a thousand different pockets, and not even Paul knew what was in all of them."

Striking a Delicate Balance

In 1915 Paul won a statewide written exam for a four-year scholarship to Rutgers University in New Jersey. Only two Black students before him had ever been enrolled at the college. (Princeton University, in Paul's hometown, would not admit them until the 1940s.)

A few other Black students were scattered at colleges along the East Coast. Together they managed to form a social circle, relying on each other for support and sympathy—the kind of sustained understanding and intimacy that not even their most tolerant white classmates offered. Paul's many achievements at Rutgers would win him respect from some white students, but never close friendship.

During his freshman year, before his abilities were fully known, Paul was more likely to find harassment than respect. When he tried out for the football squad, his teammates piled on him with such force that they left him with a broken nose, a sprained shoulder, and multiple cuts and bruises. Robeson swallowed his rage, as his father had taught him, but the furious coach—a white New Englander committed to racial equality— let the other players know that anyone who tried to injure Robeson would be immediately dropped from the team.

Several southern universities, indignant that a Black man

Paul Robeson in his full Rutgers football uniform

had been allowed to become part of the team, canceled plans to play Rutgers. Yet by his junior year Robeson had not only made the starting lineup but performed so splendidly that Walter Camp, a legendary college football coach, named him to his famed All-American football teams in 1917 and 1918. Remarkably, Paul won fifteen varsity letters in four other sports as well (basketball, baseball, javelin, and the discus throw).

In the classroom the story was much the same. Paul maintained such a high grade average that in his junior year he was one of four in a class of eighty who were admitted to Phi Beta Kappa, a society for honor students. Once his remarkable bass-baritone singing voice was discovered, he also became the lead soloist in the campus glee club—although not invited to the social functions that followed each performance or to become a "traveling" member when the club sang outside the campus. To top off Paul's multiple achievements, he became the star of the varsity debating team and won the class prize for oratory, or speech making, four years in a row.

Toward the close of his senior year, Paul was selected class valedictorian, an honor usually awarded to the student with the best academic record. His valedictory address to the senior class at graduation reflected the conflicting views then current among Black Americans about how best to improve their status.

The primary tone of the speech was pleasing and polite, echoing the views of educator and author Booker T. Washington, who'd been the leading spokesperson of the Black community for years. Washington emphasized the need for Black people to prove themselves worthy by practicing "the virtues of self-reliance, self-respect, industry, perseverance, and economy." Patiently show that we can be good citizens, Washington counseled, and we will be rewarded with full citizenship.

Yet Paul closed his speech with words closer in spirit to scholar and activist W.E.B. DuBois, one of the founders of the National Association for the Advancement of Colored People (NAACP) and a rising young challenger to Washington's gospel of humility. Sounding more like DuBois than Washington, Paul challenged his white audience "to fight for . . . an ideal government" whereby "character shall be the standard of excellence . . .

where an injury to the meanest citizen is an insult to the whole constitution."

Paul did not believe, as Washington did, that quietly submitting to a secondary status, coupled with hard and uncomplaining work and an appeal to conscience, would be enough to dissolve the country's ingrained racism. Nor did he believe that progress was inevitable, that it was bound to come in time. Like many activists of the present day, Paul believed that social change would come about only when enough people demanded it.

He had long expressed those views much more boldly when among his social circle of fellow Black college students. His girlfriend at the time, Gerry Neale, remembered many years later that among their friends Paul was the one most "aware and disturbed" about the harsh discrimination Black people faced. He took the lead in "profound discussions about the Negro in our society," in urging the others to use their education to help those less fortunate.

Paul's father, after all, had instilled in him a sense of duty to devote his gifts to "the betterment of the race." It was not yet clear to twenty-year-old Paul how he might best do so, but his commencement speech, however polite in tone, revealed the underlying urgency he felt about helping to create a more egalitarian society and putting an end to second-class citizenship. That urgency would grow stronger with the years.

Chapter 2

NEW ROLES IN PRIVATE AND PUBLIC LIFE

SHORTLY BEFORE PAUL GRADUATED FROM RUTGERS in 1919, his father unexpectedly died at age seventy-three. The Reverend Robeson had wanted Paul to become a minister, and for a time he'd felt the same. Yet after graduating he decided that a career in law better served his double purpose of making a name for himself and serving his people. He applied to the Columbia University Law School in New York City, and was accepted—the only Black man in his class. For this new turn in his life, Paul moved to Harlem, a neighborhood in the northern part of Manhattan that was home to a largely Black population.

One of "Harlem's Darlings"

At the time Paul moved to Harlem, 90 percent of the Black people in the United States still lived in the South. They were legally free, but daily they experienced grinding poverty, brutally enforced segregation, and an agricultural system that technically employed Black people but in most cases bound them for life in debt.

It was a period in the country's history known as the Progressive Era, when a number of social reforms took place, though the reforms largely excluded Black people. Instead, the Supreme Court upheld the "separate but equal" treatment of Black Americans (which was rarely equal). Even as President Woodrow Wilson proudly declared that World War I (1914–18) had made the world "safe for democracy," he refused to speak out publicly against the widespread practice of lynching "uppity" Black people.

Around 1910, a slow drift had begun of Black people, desperate for a better life, moving from the rural South to the urban North. A decade later the drift had become a tidal wave dubbed "The Great Migration." The next two decades saw some two million Black Americans shift to the north. They found no promised land, but at least their lives improved somewhat. Rates of illiteracy and infant mortality among them went down, school enrollment went up, and they had some access to local politics. In addition, community institutions like the Black church and various clubs and associations provided comfort and support.

As the Black Lives Matter protests and rallies of recent years have made clear to everyone, the Great Migration hardly solved the problem of racism in America. Black people who came north a century ago—many of them to settle in cities that are now centers of antiracist activism—found fierce resistance among Northern whites to integration in their towns and neighborhoods. The "Red Summer" of 1919 saw a series of violent white rampages that included a two-day riot in the nation's capital that injured a hundred people, mostly Black. Yet that same summer also saw a high-spirited demobilization in Harlem of Black officers and men, smartly dressed in khaki and Sam Browne belts, as they left the military after the war. Characterized by the term favored by most Black people of the time, Harlem came to be known as the Negro capital of the world. It was the cultural site of an artistic and literary Renaissance that represented the proud and assertive New Negro W.E.B. DuBois had urged.

Robeson's reputation as a multitalented star of sports, song, and scholarship had reached Harlem even before he did, and he instantly became one of "Harlem's darlings." He was frequently seen in the lively spots, usually with a pretty woman on his arm and accompanied by his two closest buddies: Jimmy Lightfoot, a musician, and Bud Fisher, a writer who was about to enroll in the Howard University College of Medicine.

Robeson's football coach at Rutgers helped to pay for his law school tuition, and Paul earned additional money from part-time coaching and playing professional football. During one game he was seriously injured and needed an emergency operation at New York City's Presbyterian Hospital. The operation was a success, but Robeson had to remain in the hospital for a number of weeks.

The patient soon grew bored, but the surgeon hit upon a solution. He brought to Paul's bedside a young Black woman named Eslanda Goode who worked as a pathology technician at the hospital. The doctor had been struck by "Essie's" (as she was called) good looks, keen intelligence, and energetic efficiency.

As for Essie, she had admired Paul at a distance at various Harlem parties and dances, and, as she later wrote, had "marked him and stored him away."

The introduction was a success: Essie and Paul immediately took to each other. In part, it was "opposites attracting"—where Robeson was natural, casual, and laid-back, Essie was more brisk and purposeful. The doctor who'd introduced them later said that Paul was quietly ambitious, Essie aggressively so: "He let things happen, she tried to make them happen."

Perhaps because of these differences, their courtship was gradual. Essie knew what she wanted, but Paul was less certain. By the winter of 1920–21, though, they were spending increasing amounts of time together, and in the summer of 1921 Paul proposed. Deciding against a formal wedding, they impulsively took the interurban streetcar to Port Chester, north of New York, and went to the local town clerk. In fifteen minutes they were officially married. A few months later they made their marriage public.

Paul went back to his studies at law school, Essie to her job at the hospital lab. Determined, as Essie put it, to make "the best and most" of a husband she called "the sweetest, most intelligent, most gifted and attractive man" she'd ever known, Essie gave up her own ambition to become a doctor and devoted herself to shaping her husband's future career. With systematic thoroughness she mulled over Paul's options, and unquestionably deserves the credit for successfully steering his early course.

First Steps Onstage

While Paul was still in law school, Essie encouraged him to join a group of amateur actors. He viewed it as a lark, but several white people who had influence in the world of theater happened to catch one of the group's performances. They recommended him to the producers who were casting a play called *Taboo*, about voodoo. It was to be performed on Broadway, the center of theatrical life. Robeson's audition wowed them, and they offered him the lead role. Essie pushed him to take it, and he reluctantly gave in, though he insisted on finishing his law degree at the same time. The play was widely reviewed, and though the critics dismissed it, a number of them praised Paul's performance, calling him "a natural." Mrs. Patrick Campbell, a legendary figure of the English stage, decided to bring *Taboo* to London with Paul repeating his role. He again hesitated, but Essie was convinced that race would hold him back less in theater than in law, where years of struggle would likely end up, at best, with nothing more than "a small political job." Her argument won the day.

The 1922 London production was not a success. Still, Essie's prediction about Paul's poor prospects for a law career soon proved all too accurate. After getting his degree early in 1923, he did get a job offer from Louis William Stotesbury, a prominent Rutgers alumnus notably free of race prejudice. Yet as the only Black person in the office, Paul soon became the subject of unfriendly remarks. The breaking point came when he asked one of the secretaries in the firm to take down a memorandum and her reply included a vile racial slur.

Paul took the matter directly to Stotesbury, who was genuinely upset. The two talked over Paul's prospects, and Stotesbury felt it his duty to acknowledge that the firm's wealthy white clients were unlikely ever to agree to a Black lawyer representing their interests. Stotesbury was willing to consider opening a Harlem branch of the firm with Paul in charge, but Robeson decided to resign instead. As he later put it, he could never have entered "any profession where the highest prizes were from the start denied me." And that was that. Paul never took the bar exam, which qualifies lawyers to practice their profession. Paul, as he would do many times in the years to come, had refused to bend his principles for the sake of making his life easier.

Confident that "something will turn up," following his instinct not to commit to something he didn't believe in, Paul let himself drift for a few months, holding himself in readiness. It was a shrewd decision. Early in 1923 he was approached by the director of the celebrated Provincetown Players to read for a role in Eugene O'Neill's new play, *All God's Chillun Got Wings*.

The Provincetown Playhouse of Cape Cod, Massachusetts, was then the country's most innovative theatrical group. O'Neill was its most distinguished playwright, and the role Paul read for was the lead. His audition was a complete success. One Provincetown Player later said that his "marvelous, incredible voice . . . was flabbergastingly impressive." He got the part.

Even before the play opened, word began to spread about the phenomenal new actor and his "marvelous" voice. Offers began to flow in. A record company approached him; the Harlem

Ethiopian Art Theatre asked about his availability; the Brooklyn YWCA invited him to perform an evening of "songs by Negro composers and authors." And before rehearsals started for *All God's Chillun Got Wings*, Paul took over the lead role—as a Black preacher in the South—for a short revival of a play called *Roseanne*. The production had an all-Black cast, but that had not been true originally; when the play had first been staged just a year earlier, it was with a cast that was entirely white—the actors had darkened their faces with burned cork. This practice, called blackface, is now scorned, but it was still widespread in the early years of Robeson's career.

Then, during the rehearsal period for *Chillun*, word spread that the play's theme was interracial marriage. Angry protests and threats from racial "purists" quickly mounted. The uproar became so intense that one newspaper predicted a race riot if the mayor of New York allowed the play to open. The Province-towners refused to bow, but the company did have to postpone the opening for four weeks due to the illness of the play's leading actress, Mary Blair.

To cover the scheduling gap, the theater decided to bring back for a week an earlier O'Neill play called *The Emperor Jones*, with Paul in the starring role, a Black American man who escapes from jail and becomes the ruler of a Caribbean island. For Robeson this was an astonishing double opportunity—and burden. Even as he continued final rehearsals for *Chillun*, he had to memorize, rehearse, and then perform the second O'Neill play as well. Somehow he carried it off. The *New York Times* hailed his performance as the Emperor Jones as "singularly fine," and the *New York Evening Graphic* declared that he "portrays the part ideally."

Two weeks later, *Chillun* opened. On the night of the premiere, police ringed the theater in anticipation of a riot. (Paul later said that he'd gone onstage half expecting "to hear shots from the stalls.") None of the expected trouble materialized. The play itself got a lukewarm reception, but Paul's performance was widely praised. One paper said that he had "superbly embodied and fully comprehended" his role. The success propelled Paul overnight into the front rank of Black American artists.

New Triumphs

Paul's acting had been highly praised, but income remained a problem—he earned only $1,782.15 from Provincetown for the entire year of 1924. Essie had to hold on to her job at the hospital lab as their chief source of income. Still, Paul had definitely "arrived." He had not only proven himself artistically but was soon being introduced to the movers and shakers in the Black literary, artistic, and political communities.

Among his new acquaintances were Gladys and Walter White. White was a member of the NAACP and would later lead the organization for decades. The couple was at the center of an interracial network of cultural figures and political activists that also included James Weldon Johnson, a prominent lawyer, editor, writer, and cultural critic.

Politically, White and Johnson held optimistic, assimilationist views that were at odds with those of the separatist Black leader Marcus Garvey, who felt that Black people should not focus on being accepted by whites but should achieve success independently of them, within their own communities. White and Johnson were also at odds with the socialism of W.E.B. DuBois, who was gaining in prominence. Robeson would later move in the direction of DuBois, but, for now, flush with his successful entrance into white artistic circles, he was not yet alienated from White and Johnson's moderate views. At this point in his life he still believed that racial barriers could be penetrated and that opportunities existed for those who were talented and determined enough to take advantage of them. Like most of the artists of the Harlem Renaissance, he was convinced that art would prove stronger than prejudice.

Paul and Essie's social life rapidly expanded. Before long Carl Van Vechten, the white champion of the Black literary renaissance and his actor wife, brought the Robesons into what seemed like a nonstop round of glamorous interracial parties. They raised glasses with, among the celebrated figures of the day, composer George Gershwin; writers Theodore Dreiser, Sherwood Anderson, Jessie Fauset, and Countee Cullen; and the dancer Adele Astaire. Sometimes a group of partygoers would go on to catch a midnight show at one of the current Harlem hot spots like the Club Alabam or to dance to Fletcher Henderson's big band, the Rainbow Orchestra. It was a heady life.

In between the rounds of parties, Paul found time to meet with agents and to perform an occasional concert, including one at the NAACP's annual event of 1924. His first formal concert, arranged by a white socialite, consisted entirely of Black spirituals, songs that originated among enslaved Black people in the American South and were based on an oral tradition invoking

Black America's First Major Moviemaker

Body and Soul, Paul Robeson's first movie, was a "race film"—one of five hundred or so movies made in the United States between about 1915 and the 1950s with Black casts for Black audiences. Although many were written, directed, financed, and produced by white individuals and companies, *Body and Soul* was entirely the work of Oscar Micheaux, now recognized as the first major Black filmmaker in the United States.

Like Robeson, Micheaux was the son of a man who'd been born into slavery. At an early age, he set out on his own to make his way in the world. He found work on the railroads as a Pullman porter, working as an attendant in the sleeping cars. For many years this was one of the better-paying and secure jobs for Black men, and it allowed Micheaux to travel and to save money. He then homesteaded on land he bought in South Dakota, surrounded mostly by white neighbors. That experience gave him the material for a novel that, in 1919, became his first movie.

Before his death in 1951, Micheaux made more than forty race films, in addition to writing seven books. His work was notable for portraying well-rounded Black characters dealing with the problems of contemporary life. He has been recognized with a star on the Hollywood Walk of Fame, a special award from the Directors Guild of America, and a commemorative postage stamp, among other honors.

the hardships of slavery while also often conveying Christian values. The concert took place in November 1924 at the Copley Plaza Hotel in Boston. Later that same year, the famous Black filmmaker Oscar Micheaux gave Paul his first movie role. The film was *Body and Soul*, the story of a corrupt pastor and his noble brother, and Paul was signed to play both parts. Essie drew up the contract and proved her negotiating skill, getting a percentage of the film's earnings. Paul carried off his double role with equal assurance, projecting a powerfully charismatic film presence.

An even more important professional development lay directly ahead: Paul started to work with Larry Brown, a talented gay man who was known as a superb arranger of Black spirituals and work songs. Robeson and Brown had earlier met briefly, and now they decided to join forces professionally. Carl Van Vechten arranged a public concert for April 1925 and spread the word among the "smart set" that the event was not to be missed.

Even standing room was sold out by the night of the concert, with hundreds gathered on the sidewalk outside the theater clamoring for seats. Applause at the end was thunderous, and the audience demanded encore after encore until the management had to turn up the houselights to persuade the crowd to leave.

The next day critics confirmed the event as a triumph and a milestone. The concert marked the first time a Black soloist— rather than a choral group like the famed Fisk Jubilee Singers— had devoted an entire evening to Black spirituals and work songs. One reviewer hailed Robeson as "the embodiment of the aspirations of the New Negro." Robeson, the reviewer said, was "destined to be the new American Caruso"—a reference to the famous opera star Enrico Caruso.

The concert proved a watershed event for Robeson. A tidal wave of offers rolled in from agents, tour managers, churches, film producers, clubs, concert halls, and recording companies. The Victor Talking Machine Company was willing to guarantee "not less than three double-faced records." Equity, the actors' guild, wanted him to appear at its annual dinner. The magazine *Vanity Fair* wanted him to sit for pictures. The renowned producer David Belasco wanted him to co-star on Broadway in a new play—and so on.

Paul, for starters, chose to repeat his role in *The Emperor Jones*, this time in a production in London. He and Essie found an ideal flat in the city's Chelsea neighborhood, and Essie wrote in her diary that it was "beautifully furnished in the most exquisite taste," with "fireplaces in all the rooms."

The Robesons also found in London what Essie described as a "warm, friendly and unprejudiced" reception. Years earlier, when Paul was rehearsing *The Emperor Jones* in Greenwich Village—known as the freewheeling and liberal part of New York—the nearest and only place he could get a decent meal was many blocks north at Penn Station; the next nearest place was Harlem. In London, dozens of attractive restaurants near the theater welcomed him warmly.

He and Essie were free from other humiliations as well. White theaters in New York would sell only balcony seats to Black customers; on Pullman trains Black passengers could buy only the noisy seats over the wheels; and white hotels refused them rooms outright. London provided a welcome change from

*Paul Robeson in the 1925 London
production of* The Emperor Jones

these indignities, even if it was not, as the Robesons would later discover, as free from prejudice as they first imagined.

Opening night of *The Emperor Jones* was a gala event. A glamorous audience filled every seat. One of those seats was occupied by the Robesons' favorite new friend, the famed anarchist Emma Goldman, who'd been forced to leave the United States for her political beliefs, which the authorities claimed were dangerously revolutionary.

Reviews for the play itself were mixed, but Paul received raves for his powerful performance. The next day he was besieged by reporters, and by three in the afternoon he had already given six interviews. The theater put Paul's name up in lights on the huge electric sign at Cambridge Circus. And the Robesons' social calendar quickly filled, with one event standing out above the others: Miss Amanda Ira Aldridge, the daughter of great nineteenth-century Black actor Ira Aldridge, had seen the play and wrote to thank Paul for his "magnificent performance." The two spent an afternoon together, during which she presented him with the earrings her father had worn onstage as the star of Shakespeare's *Othello*. She hoped, she said, that Paul, too, would one day wear them when playing the role.

Chapter 3

A CAREER TAKES FLIGHT

FOLLOWING PAUL'S HUGE SUCCESS IN LONDON, THE Robesons took a long vacation in France, the start of years of international travel for both of them. Then they returned to the States, where Paul and Larry Brown went on their first concert tour and released their first recordings. Both ventures were successful.

Amidst all the professional success and acclaim, Paul had grown increasingly unhappy in his marriage. He deeply appreciated Essie's business instincts, and he knew how much her managerial skills had contributed to his professional success. In that sense, the difference in their temperaments had been an advantage, but it also had a negative side. Paul's deep sensuality had never matched up well with Essie's less passionate nature, and, in addition, Paul refused to conform to the mainstream culture's norm of monogamy, the idea that people should limit themselves throughout their lives to a single sexual partner. A turning point had come in 1923, when Paul met Freda Diamond, a young Russian Jewish beauty. She and Paul began an on-and-off affair that would continue until Paul—by then

Paul and Essie Robeson arrive in Manhattan
after a successful European tour, 1935

enamored of the actress Uta Hagen—put an end to it in the early 1940s.

Throughout the coming years, Essie would react to Paul's love affairs in ways that ranged from anger to indifference. But she did want to remain "Mrs. Robeson," and although she herself once suggested divorce, that was an isolated and fleeting impulse.

Parenthood

In 1927 Essie gave birth to a son, Paul Robeson Jr. (nicknamed Pauli). Paul's distaste for domestic life, however, did not lessen. He preferred the company of adults and would never be more than a distant parent. Pauli was never able to engage his father's lasting interest or approval. Essie was the more consistent parent of the two, though not a selfless one devoted entirely to her child, as was then expected of mothers. She was a feminist ahead of her time, a woman who felt entitled to her own ambition. For several years during the 1930s, Essie's stern mother, Ma Goode, would be Pauli's primary caregiver, and he would see his parents infrequently.

At the time Essie gave birth, Paul—at her insistence—remained in Europe to complete a highly successful concert tour. When Essie developed medical complications from the birth, she concealed the truth from Paul, not wanting him to interrupt the tour. Her condition worsened, however, and Ma Goode took it upon herself to notify Paul. He returned at once to the States.

During Essie's slow recovery, Paul was entirely attentive to her needs. Only when she was well along in recovery and could travel did he accept his next major stage role.

Paul and Paul Jr. in London, 1936

Black Identity in the Arts

Florenz Ziegfeld Jr., a leading producer of theatrical shows, offered Paul the part of Joe in the London production of *Show Boat*. This American musical about entertainers on a Mississippi riverboat had already been a runaway hit in New York. The London version, too, became a success, though Paul's performance impressed the leading critics far more than the show itself did. James Agate, the most prestigious London critic of the day, went so far as to suggest that the producers cut a half hour out of the "inept and clumsy" show and fill it in with Robeson singing spirituals.

A number of Black intellectuals, however, were much less enthusiastic. One of them was J.A. Rogers, the highly regarded European correspondent for the *New York Amsterdam News*, a leading Black paper. He criticized Robeson's character Joe as being simply one more instance of the "lazy, good-natured, lolling darkey" stereotype "that exists more in white men's fancy than in reality."

But a Black actor had few options. It was primarily a choice of playing such roles or giving up acting entirely. Besides—though Paul would never say so in public, aware that he'd be seen as bragging—the warm humanity he communicated in the role of Joe did something to soften the stereotype. In any case, as Paul grew increasingly political over the next decade, he would periodically take it upon himself—without consulting *Show Boat's* writer, Oscar Hammerstein—to change some of the lyrics that Joe sang. By the time a film of *Show Boat* was made in 1935, for example, Robeson had changed "I'm tired of livin' and scared of dyin'" in the song "Ol' Man River" to "I must keep fightin' until I'm dyin'."

During the yearlong London run of *Show Boat*, Paul grew "bored to death" with the role of Joe. In preparation for the show's eventual closing, he filled in his time with voice and French lessons, along with coaching in German that allowed him to begin to add material from Mozart's opera *The Magic Flute* to his repertoire. He and Larry Brown also signed up with the prestigious Celebrity Concert Tour.

Paul, Essie, and Paul Robeson Jr.

Essie joined Paul in London after *Show Boat* opened, and in time the Robesons brought over Paul Jr. and Essie's mother, Ma Goode, from the States as well. They rented a house that came complete with servants, where they hosted a grand party for the crowd of prominent people they'd met in London as well as a few of their American friends who were in town. The Van Vechtens were the guests of honor, and the next day Carl Van Vechten wrote in a letter, "Paul sang and was a lamb. It was their first party and a great success."

By the time *Show Boat* closed its doors in March 1929, a concert tour had already been booked for Paul and Larry. It extended to Vienna, Austria; Prague, in what is now the Czech Republic; and Budapest, Hungary. The demand for tickets was so great that second concerts had to be added in every city.

In Budapest Robeson was struck by the similarities he saw between the Black spirituals and the folk songs of the Roma people, who were then called Gypsies. This marked the beginning of his keen interest in charting universal patterns in the folk music of widely different cultures. Robeson's interest in Africa, too, had just begun to emerge. He was especially delighted when a Polish musician "proved" to him that "the melodies of Central Africa have also influenced European music" and "traced its descent through the Moors [North Africans] and the Spaniards until it reached Poland." The theory captivated Robeson and would become something of an obsession in the years ahead.

Chapter 4

DRAMA ON AND
OFF THE STAGE

IT HAD LONG BEEN IN ROBESON'S MIND TO SOMEDAY
take on the role of Othello in Shakespeare's play, which carries
the subtitle *The Moor of Venice*, referring to the Moorish origin
of its Black title character. By 1930 the idea had entered other
minds as well.

A producer named Maurice Browne and his wife, director Nellie Van Volkenburg, offered Robeson a contract for the
role of Othello. Rumor said it was the largest sum ever paid
in London for a nonmusical role. They also hired the brilliant
twenty-two-year-old newcomer Peggy Ashcroft to play opposite
Robeson as Desdemona, his wife. The cast also included Ralph
Richardson, a future star, and Sybil Thorndike, one of the great
figures of the London stage. Browne had promised Robeson a
"first-rate" actor in the role of Iago, the scheming villain of the
play, but vanity overruled his judgment. He decided to play the
role himself—despite limited acting experience. To make things
worse, he then appointed his wife to direct the play, although
she had no experience with Shakespeare.

Just before the start of rehearsals a nasty racial incident

changed the Robesons' high opinion of London. They were invited to join friends for late-night drinks at the Savoy Grill, the posh watering hole of the supposedly color-blind upper class. The waiter, however, told the Robesons that he could not allow them in the dining room. Paul was astonished and thought there must be some mistake, since he and Essie had dined at the Savoy many times. He sent for the manager, thinking he would surely set things right. Not at all. The manager told Paul that the management had recently changed its policy: it no longer permitted Negroes to enter the Grill.

News of the insult leaked out to the newspapers and created a considerable stir. Only a month before, Robeson had told a reporter that in London, "the colour problem exists only with illiterate English people." His eyes were further opened when a number of Africans and West Indians living in London called a protest meeting where recent discriminatory actions against people of color were discussed. The Savoy incident was also brought up in the House of Commons, part of Britain's legislature. Prime Minister Ramsay MacDonald—who the previous year had entertained Robeson there—announced that the Savoy's ban on Black people "is not in accordance with our British hotel practice, but I cannot think of any way in which the Government can intervene."

Paul chose to believe that "the influence of American race prejudice was responsible for the affront." But within a few short years, after his political education had deepened, he came to recognize that the British taste for imperial rule over "colored people" needed no outside encouragement.

A Muddled *Moor of Venice*

At the start of rehearsals for *Othello,* Essie predicted that "we are going to have a magnificent time." It proved anything but. Paul realized almost immediately that both his director and his Iago were hopelessly inept and likely to hinder the play's success.

Essie, too, soon realized that her prediction was way off the mark. "[Director] Nellie doesn't know what it is all about," she wrote in her diary. She "talks a lot of parlor junk" about "the tapestry of the scene" and "the psychological dimensions" of the play, but "can't even get actors from one side of the stage to the other. Poor Paul," she added, "is lost."

Nellie's idea of directing was to stand at the back of the theater and yell instructions through a megaphone. She reacted to Paul's questions as if he were a naughty superstar asking for special treatment—which was very nearly the opposite of his temperament. At one point, when he asked Nellie a specific question about where he should be standing during a particular moment in the play, she responded through her megaphone, "There are other people on the stage besides yourself, Mr. Robeson!" A horrified Peggy Ashcroft drew the inescapable conclusion that Nellie was "a racist." Peggy, in turn, was constantly being asked by reporters if, as a young white woman, she "minded being kissed in some of the scenes by a coloured man." She developed a stock response: "Of course I do not mind! I look on it as a privilege to act with such a great artist like Paul Robeson."

The press bombarded the cast with questions about "how the public will take to seeing a Negro make love to a white woman."

*Paul Robeson and Peggy Ashcroft, his co-star
in* Othello *and brief love interest*

They made Paul feel so skittish that he later revealed that "for the first two weeks in every scene I played with Desdemona that girl couldn't get near to me. I was backing away from her all the time. I was like a plantation hand in the parlor, that clumsy." He and the other actors, except Browne in the role of Iago, soon decided that Nellie was more of a hindrance than a help. They secretly met in the evenings to rehearse in one another's homes.

Nellie, however, retained final control of staging, lights, and sets, and she managed to make a considerable botch of all three. She made ill-advised cuts in the text and put much of the stage action as far as possible from the audience, staging the final scene of the play, in which Othello kills Desdemona while she is sleeping, with the bed tucked far away in a corner. To make matters worse, the bed caused a racket when being hoisted into position behind the curtain during the crucial scene before Desdemona's death.

Nellie also kept the lighting so dim throughout the play that the actors actually had trouble seeing each other. Ralph Richardson kept a flashlight up his sleeve to light his way across the stage. To top off her miscalculations, Nellie dressed Robeson not in appropriate, dignified Moorish robes but in unsuitable Elizabethan tights, with puffed sleeves and doublets.

By opening night, as Essie reported, Paul was "wild with nerves." He felt that he started off his performance at too high a pitch and only settled down as he went along. Yet the gala audience called him back at the close for twenty curtain calls, and the critics were kinder than expected. Nellie Van Volkenburg's direction and Maurice Browne's performance as Iago got the drubbing they deserved, but Sybil Thorndike came off well and Ashcroft got raves. Robeson's reviews ran the gamut from "magnificent" to "prosaic" and "disappointing." A few of the critics struck an unmistakably racist note, with one declaring that Robeson's overly "cautious" approach to the role had been due not to personal modesty but to his fear that any "assumption of arrogance might be mistaken for the insolent assumptions of the less educated of his race." Ticket sales were modest, and the show closed in six weeks.

There had been talk of bringing *Othello* to the States, but nobody wanted Maurice Browne's badly flawed production. He, in turn, claimed that he alone had the right to "sell" Robeson for any other restaged version. There was also apprehension, which Paul shared, about how American audiences would receive a Black man amorously kissing a white woman onstage. He told a *New York Times* reporter that "the audience would get rough; in fact, might become very dangerous." One southern newspaper spoke for many when it confirmed Paul's fears: "He knows what would happen and so do the rest of us. That is one form of amusement that we will not stand for now or ever. This negro has potentialities for great harm to his race."

A Tangled Love Life

Career matters, in any case, soon took a backseat to personal ones. Essie discovered that Paul and Peggy Ashcroft had been having an affair. Essie wasn't exactly surprised, but she was enraged. She knew that Paul had no intention of remaining monogamous and had had previous affairs, but Peggy hit a special nerve: Essie had described her in her diary as a "lovely girl." She now denounced Ashcroft for "setting her sights on somebody else's husband." As for Paul, Essie accused him of being "a smooth one" and said that "his personality is built on lies."

In the face of Essie's fury, Paul remained calm. He wrote her a straightforward account of what she could expect from him in the future: "It must be quite evident that I'm likely to go on thusly [that is, nonmonogamously] for a long while here and there—perhaps not. . . . I must have a certain amount of privacy in my life. . . . I would like to get on with my work. To do that I think I need to be alone and to be as far as possible absolutely free. . . . I'm sure that deep down I love you very much in the way that we could love each other. It could not be wholly complete because we are too different in temperament. . . . Something's wrong—maybe my fault, maybe yours—most likely both our faults. . . . Write me always as you feel. . . . Let's hope all will come out right."

Instead of calming Essie, Paul's letter made her still angrier. She characterized it in her diary as "cold, mean, vindictive," and added, "He excuses himself with high sounding words that merely mask a disgusting commonness. We will begin from here."

The affair with Peggy Ashcroft was soon over. But within a short time, Paul became far more seriously involved with another woman, Yolande Jackson, an actress who was the daughter of a prominent lawyer. Ever after Robeson described her to close friends as "the great love" of his life.

Paul soon told Essie about his consuming passion for Yolande and asked for a divorce. Coming so soon after the affair with Peggy Ashcroft, the news hit Essie hard, and she had something like a nervous collapse. "I have been terribly ill with nerves," she wrote to her old friends the Van Vechtens—so ill that a form of paralysis set in on the left side of her face. The doctors told her that it might be permanent.

But Essie was tough and resilient. Within a few months she had come to terms with the bad hand she'd been dealt. Her health improved, she began to go out more and to see friends, and she agreed with Paul that they should live separately until they could reach some sort of agreement about the future. Essie chose to believe that Paul would decide against a divorce and that the affair with Yolande would soon blow over.

As she would soon learn, that was wishful thinking. Paul had made up his mind to divorce Essie and to marry Yolande. "Paul is behaving very, very strangely," Essie wrote the Van Vechtens. "He can't seem to make up his mind what to do about . . . anything." In her businesslike manner, she set out to clear the air. She wrote Paul that she was perfectly willing to give him a divorce.

She accused him, though, of continuing to drift. If he was ever to realize his full potential, she told him, he needed to work hard at his profession, to draw up a plan and stick to it. Rather than respond with accusations of his own, Paul continued to play his cards close to the vest. He simply reassured Essie that whatever the outcome, he was certain they would always remain close and friendly.

The stalemate continued throughout 1931. After a successful concert tour in the States, for which he received excellent reviews, Paul joined Yolande in Europe for a vacation. He then returned to the United States for a revival of *Show Boat*. Critics gave it high praise; the *New York Times* declared that it was "the most beautifully blended musical show we have had in this country."

At this point, Paul finally asked Essie to begin divorce proceedings. "I'm glad to have it over with at last," Essie wrote in her diary. To the press, Paul confirmed the long-standing rumor that the Robesons were divorcing, emphasizing that they had been separated for two years and that the parting was friendly. He also confirmed that he'd been seeing an Englishwoman, but he refused to reveal her identity. He did make it clear that she was white and told the press that he was "prepared to leave the United States if there is any stir about it. I desire above all things to maintain my personal dignity and will tolerate no racial abuse."

Essie was determined to put the best face on the divorce. She even wrote an article on divorce in which she claimed the "enlightened" view that not all marriages should last forever; when they reached a natural ending point, the parting should be cordial and without blame. Privately, Essie predicted to close friends that Paul was "going to have a horrible time" and claimed to feel "terribly sorry for him." She gloried in the rumors that Paul, in New York with *Show Boat*, was "depressed and unhappy."

He was not. Not remotely. *Show Boat* continued to be a megahit. He was still adored in Harlem. He was studying French, Russian, and German. His concert to a sold-out crowd at the stadium of New York's City College was greeted rapturously by the critics. And his alma mater, Rutgers University, awarded him an honorary Master of Arts degree. Robeson particularly savored the irony of being cited along with the president of Princeton, which still barred its gates to Black students.

Paul returned to England in the late summer of 1932 believing that divorce proceedings were well along. He had hired a business manager named Bob Rockmore to replace Essie in that role, and his new life with Yolande was about to begin with a yearlong holiday in France. And then it happened: word arrived from Yolande that she was calling off their plans to marry. Paul's cloudless sky abruptly darkened.

He was devastated. One close friend worried that he might

kill himself. But Robeson attempted to keep up a good front, steeled himself to fulfill his contracts, and tried to understand what had gone wrong. If he ever found out, he never passed the information along. All that is known for certain is that several months after Yolande abandoned him, Paul told Essie to stop divorce proceedings. He again began to spend time with her and Pauli, and before long he moved into their apartment. The rumor mill had a field day with various theories about the breakup with Yolande, but none can be confirmed.

She and Paul stayed in touch for at least another twenty years, with Larry Brown serving as the main go-between. A dozen letters have been found, including several from Yolande, covering the years 1932–53. They reveal a continuing, though secret, attachment between Paul and Yolande, along with occasional contact. The letters suggest, too, that over time Yolande came to regret her decision not to marry Paul. As late as 1950, she confessed in a letter to Larry Brown that her separation from Paul was "eating into my soul."

Back to Essie and Work

The Robesons put together a new version of their marriage. They did so on Paul's terms; though he would never again propose marriage to any woman with whom he became involved, he did have several significant relationships in the years ahead. For now, with the wrenching three-year affair with Yolande still fresh, Paul was content to retreat to *his* version of domesticity and to plunge back into work.

First up on Paul's new agenda was a London production of Eugene O'Neill's *All God's Chillun Got Wings*, Robeson's favorite role. He was blessed with a brilliant co-star, Flora Robson, and a gifted director, André Van Gyseghem. Both of them found Paul a joy to work with. Van Gyseghem later said that "he was not up on a throne but a real human person that you could contact," considerate of the other actors, easy to approach, and open to direction.

Flora Robson, too, was smitten with Paul as a person, though she agreed with his own modest assessment that he lacked "technique." His movement was occasionally awkward, and he sometimes declaimed his lines as though making a speech rather than speaking naturally. As she put it, Paul acted from instinct; if he didn't *feel* a line or a speech, he couldn't persuasively convey it to an audience. In *All God's Chillun*, Paul played an unsure but sincere young man, which meant that his shortcomings as an actor beautifully fit the awkwardness of this particular character. As a result, the reviews were nearly all positive.

Immediately following the success of *Chillun*, Paul and Essie left for New York, where they stayed in separate living quarters. He returned to his role in *The Emperor Jones*—but on film this time. The movie was made at Paramount's Astoria Studios on Long Island. It was Robeson's first talkie and first commercial film, and its budget of a quarter of a million dollars was high for the time.

All went smoothly, and shooting was completed in just thirty-eight days. But trouble came from an unexpected quarter. The movie industry's censoring agency, the Hays Office, insisted that the kissing scene between Robeson and his black co-star

Paul Robeson and co-star Fredi Washington
in The Emperor Jones, *1933*

Fredi Washington had to be filmed over again. The problem, the Hays Office declared, was that the light-skinned Washington looked like a white woman on-screen. Interracial lovemaking was taboo. The producers reluctantly reshot the scene—taking care to apply dark makeup to Fredi Washington's face.

On the film's release, a different complaint came from another direction. A number of Black intellectuals and newspapers criticized Robeson for performing the stereotype, as one of them put it, of the Black man as "essentially craven . . . a miserable victim to moral breakdown and superstitious fears."

In public interviews, Robeson himself indirectly sided with the film's critics. Hollywood, he told one reporter, "can only realize the plantation type of Negro—the Negro of 'poor Old Joe' and 'Swanee Ribber.'" It was unlikely, he told a British reporter, to take on the stories of "the great Negro emperors—Menelik, Chaka," though he'd love to play the roles of those African leaders. The United States, he added, "would hardly believe that there had ever been such a person as a great Negro emperor, but in England you know it. You have had to conquer one or two."

Chapter 5

DISCOVERING AFRICA

ROBESON'S SHARP REMARK ABOUT AFRICAN EMPER-
ors who had fought back against British imperial conquest accurately revealed Robeson's rising political awareness during the
early 1930s. His growing interest in Africa developed alongside
his expanding criticism of the United States and of white Western values in general.

Becoming Bolder

In a 1933 interview with *Film Weekly*, Robeson claimed that
much of what was distinctive in American culture—especially
in music—came from Black sources. "We are a great race," he
told another reporter, "greater in tradition and culture than the
American race. Why should we copy something that's inferior?"

This was a far more radical statement than anything Robeson had previously said publicly. Other papers picked up his
remarks, and he was asked if he'd been accurately reported. "A
trifle exaggerated," he slyly replied. In the early 1930s, however,
Robeson spoke out boldly only now and then. As he put it to
yet another reporter, "I am proud of my African descent, but I

am very far from being color-conscious. . . . I am essentially an artist and a cosmopolitan."

Before long, though, Robeson's boldness would become more frequent. He began an energetic study of African history and culture, and he even enrolled in London's School of Oriental Studies to learn more about African languages. He increasingly came to believe that the special gifts and values of Black people represented an approach to life that united them even as it set them apart from white Westerners.

As Robeson's studies deepened, he met a number of young Africans who were living and studying in London. Among them were several future leaders of their countries, including Jomo Kenyatta of Kenya and Kwame Nkrumah of Ghana. He also got to know the radical Caribbean intellectual C.L.R. James, who was a socialist and a supporter of the idea that a nation's resources and its means of creating wealth should be shared equally by all citizens. James also supported independence for the Caribbean islands that had long since been claimed and colonized by Europeans. He and Robeson would connect again a few years later.

As time went on, Robeson's study of phonetics—the sounds of speech—led him to believe that there was "a kinship of rhythm and intonation" between the varied African languages and contemporary Black dialect. He became so enthusiastic about his discoveries that he began to talk of visiting Africa, even of settling there eventually.

As his excitement grew, he began jotting down his ideas in shorthand. Black people in the United States, he wrote, had already become Westernized, "American to the core." As he saw it, only three possibilities remained: First, for Black Americans to "give up and disappear as a race altogether," which to him was a "spineless," unthinkable outcome. Second, for them to remain an oppressed, servile group, also unthinkable. Or, third, Black people could become "a self-respecting, solid racial unit—with its spiritual roots back in Africa," so highly developed that no one could deny their equality with white people.

In formulating these alternatives, Robeson rejected the kind of Black nationalism that called for a literal return to Africa—the solution of Marcus Garvey and, later, the Nation of Islam. He also rejected the assimilationism that he felt the NAACP represented by encouraging Black people to seek acceptance within mainstream culture. Even before his discovery of Africa, Robeson had never been an assimilationist, someone who champions the so-called "melting pot" in which cultural variations disappear and a new kind of human being—the "American"—emerges.

Black people, Robeson felt, should look to Africa both for their cultural roots and for their futures. The culture of contemporary Africans was, he felt, of "high quality," as shown in their music, in a complex tribal system, and in a group of languages capable of expressing "the most subtle ideas." Robeson believed that Black Africa offered a distinctive contribution to world culture.

Going a step further, Robeson wanted to combine ethnic integrity *and* international solidarity. His was a vision of humanity's future that would respect divergent folkways and at the same time borrow from them to create a truly cosmopolitan society—one that included elements from all over the world.

Robeson's political and cultural views evolved over the years. In the early 1930s he primarily emphasized the importance of a proud Black racial identity. By the late 1930s, after visiting the Soviet Union, the communist state now known as Russia, and then later witnessing the civil war against fascism in Spain, his emphasis would shift to the importance of revolutionary internationalism.

Later still, in the 1950s, after his hopes for a cosmopolitan new internationalism had been destroyed by the Cold War—a period of heightened tension, rivalry, and hostility between the United States and the Soviet Union—Robeson would again strongly identify with his own Black cultural roots. As he saw it, the core values of that identity were its sense of community, its emphasis on things of the spirit (but not religious "mythology"), and its trust in what he called "the higher intuition," something that was more than instinct or reason. To avoid the catastrophe that he believed had befallen Westernized Black people, Robeson urged young Africans to reject the fundamental values of the West. Black Africans, he argued, should borrow the West's "technique" alone, remembering that technique was "mechanical and only fit for certain uses." The goal was to borrow from the West what was useful, but not to adopt its values.

Through the years Robeson would work and rework the views that began to take shape during his time in London in the 1930s. What he tried to hold in balance throughout his life was a commitment to cultural distinctiveness *in combination with* international cosmopolitanism. He considered it essential, above all, to remember that "the human *stem* was one."

Seeking the Source

While the Robesons were in London, Paul was not alone in his deep dive into African culture. Essie pursued her own investigations into anthropology—the study of human cultures—at the London School of Economics and University College. "When we get through," she wrote to the Van Vechtens, "we will know something about 'our people.' "[6]

Both Paul and Essie read the 1934 novel *Jonah's Gourd Vine* by African American author and anthropologist Zora Neale Hurston. Essie wrote to Hurston to express their admiration and to describe the African studies she and Paul had embarked on. Hurston wrote back that the news was "thrilling." She said, "I feel so keenly that you have at last set your feet on the right road. You know that we don't know anything about ourselves. . . . I am truly happy that you and Paul are going to sources."[7] In 1936, accompanied by Pauli, Essie would spend three months traveling widely in Africa.

Politics and Performances

Robeson's evolving political and cultural views brought other changes as well. He announced to the press toward the end of 1934 that he no longer had any desire "to interpret the vocal genius of half a dozen cultures which are really alien to me." From that time on, he said, he'd drop all classical Western music from his concert programs. (He made an exception for the "intoxicating" music of Bach and Mozart.)

In the future, Robeson said, he would concentrate on presenting the folk music of the world. Folk music, he felt, was "the music of basic realities, the spontaneous expression by the people for the people of elemental emotions." In particular, he found that the folk songs of Russian, Hebrew, Eastern European, and Northern Scots people were closest to the underlying spirit of African American songs. His close kinship with Hebrew culture would lead him in 1934 to declare that the rise of the Nazis, who would go on to kill millions of Jews and others in the Holocaust, was "the most retrograde [backward] step the world has seen for centuries."

Given his shifting worldview, Robeson cast around for film roles that would foster the ideals he'd come to care most about. He thought his search was over when Alexander and Zoltán Korda, Hungarian-born brothers who had become major figures in the British film industry, offered him the leading role of Bosambo, an African chief, in a film based on the popular book *Sanders of the River* by bestselling British author Edgar Wallace.

The Kordas had already spent five months in central Africa taking 160,000 feet of film of African music, speech, dance, and ritual. When they showed Robeson the footage, he thought it "magnificent"—an absolute confirmation that Africa still had an "integrated culture unspoiled by Western influence." Enthralled, he turned down an offer from the Chicago Opera to perform the role of the Ethiopian king in *Aida* to accept the Kordas' offer to play Bosambo.

Robeson excitedly told a reporter that he expected *Sanders of the River* to be a "milestone," the first time Western audiences would experience *authentic* African culture. Alight with

Robeson as Bosambo, with actress
Nina Mae McKinney, in Sanders of the River—
a film he later viewed as a betrayal of his values

enthusiasm, he felt certain of having "found my place in the world, that there's something out of my own culture which I can express and perhaps help to preserve—for I'm not kidding myself that I've really gotten a place in Western culture, although I have been trained in it all my life."

Given Robeson's high hopes, the final version of the film was a bitter disappointment, nothing less than a defense and glorification of British imperialism. The character Bosambo was presented as the loyal lackey of his white master, and advertisements for the film explicitly described its theme as "a million mad savages fighting for one beautiful woman!—until three white comrades ALONE pitched into the fray and quelled the bloody revolt!"

Robeson claimed that "the imperialist angle" had been added to the plot in the last five days of shooting, too late for him to grasp that the original storyline had been grossly distorted. Since Robeson's contract contained no provision for him to approve the film's final cut, he felt stymied and despairing. He went so far as to offer to buy the film to prevent its release, but the Kordas rejected his offer.

The *Sunday Times* (London) review confirmed Robeson's worst fears. The paper, a champion of British imperialism, applauded *Sanders of the River* for providing "a grand insight into our special English difficulties in the governing of savage races . . . it could not be improved upon for the respect it displays to British sensibilities and ambitions."

As for *African* sensibilities, not a word was said in *The Times*—but *Black* reviewers and the Black press had plenty to say. They gave both the film and its star a thorough drubbing. The *polite* Black critics suggested that Robeson had been hoodwinked: "Here we have the pathetic spectacle," one of them wrote, "of one of the most gifted and distinguished members of his race placed in a position where in actuality he is forced into caricatures of his people." The *impolite* Black reviewers mocked Robeson's "authentic" African singing in the film, with one of them claiming that the "war song" irresistibly reminded him of the famous marching song from *The Vagabond King*, a popular romantic operetta that had been made into a film in 1930.

Sanders of the River was a commercial and popular success, perhaps *because* it glorified British imperialism. But for Robeson himself the film was a source of embarrassment and grief. He accepted full responsibility for the disaster and made a clean break with the film. The whole experience made him realize that he couldn't disentangle himself from Western values simply by wishing to do so, certainly not overnight. Of one thing he remained certain: his new dream of African liberation had been right, not wrong. He had simply looked in the wrong place for its fulfillment. The point was not to give up the dream, but to look elsewhere.

Chapter 6

NAZIS, COMMUNISTS— AND HOLLYWOOD

As if someone had been reading Robeson's thoughts, an invitation arrived from the celebrated Russian filmmaker Sergei Eisenstein asking him to come to Moscow, Russia's capital and the major city of the Soviet Union, as a guest of the Administration for Films, to discuss making a movie together. Eisenstein had long been an admirer of Black culture. For some time he'd wanted to make a film about Toussaint L'Ouverture, the Black general who liberated the Caribbean island of Haiti from French colonizers and slaveholders in the 1790s. L'Ouverture's story had long been dear to Robeson's heart as well.

The trip to Moscow would do more than bring together two of the great talents of their time. It would give Robeson firsthand experience of two systems of ideas—and the political systems related to them—that had appeared on the world stage in the first half of the twentieth century. The effect of the visit to the Soviet Union on Robeson's political thought would be profound.

Threats and Welcomes

The journey by train to Moscow required Paul and Essie to spend a daylong layover in Berlin. There Robeson came face-to-face with Nazism, the ideology that dominated Germany under the leadership of Adolf Hitler, head of the government since 1933. Like other forms of fascism, Nazism was marked by fanatical insistence on national identity and pride—the very opposite of Robeson's international perspective—and by a shift from democratic government to rule by an all-powerful dictator. A core element of Nazi ideology was the belief in white supremacy—in particular, the supremacy of Northern Europeans, whom the Nazis considered to be of "pure" Germanic blood. Jewish, Roma, and Black people were seen as innately inferior.

When the Robesons reached Berlin, Paul saw that the German metropolis was no longer the city he remembered from five years earlier, when he had played *The Emperor Jones* there and had marveled at Berlin's artistic experimentation and its lack of racial discrimination. The city was now controlled by the Nazis, and Robeson's dark skin drew persistent and hostile stares. The threatening hatred in the eyes of three storm troopers reminded him of a lynch mob. He and Essie decided to stay close to their hotel all day. After the train pulled out of the Berlin station, Paul sat hunched in a corner staring out into the darkness.

A very different reception greeted them at the Moscow railroad station. An entire delegation was waiting, headed by Sergei Eisenstein. It included Essie's brothers, John and Frank Goode, who'd earlier moved to the Soviet Union to live in what they believed was a socialist country free of racial discrimination.

Essie's brothers were not alone. Many liberal or left-wing thinkers of the day saw great promise in the Soviet Union, and hailed it as a hopeful experiment rising from the ashes of the tyrannical Russian Empire, which had been overthrown in 1917. The Soviet economy was being reorganized along socialist principles of public ownership, while its government, led by the Communist Party, declared the goal of achieving a society of full equality where everyone's basic needs would be met. The original Soviet ideals of equality and of respect for the cultural identity of all peoples powerfully appealed to Robeson, and his commitment to those ideals would shape the rest of his life— although he would pay a high professional and personal price for holding fast to them.

Following the initial reception at the railroad station, the Robesons were taken to their magnificent set of rooms in the National Hotel near Red Square. To the reporters and interviewers who crowded into their suite, Paul—who spoke Russian fluently—explained that his chief interest during their visit would be "to study the Soviet national minority policy as it operates among the peoples of Central Asia." He was referring to those regions, such as Uzbekistan and Tajikistan, that were part of the Soviet Union but were inhabited by non-Russian ethnic populations. To emphasize the point, he added, "I'm not interested in any European culture, not even the culture of Moscow—but I *am* interested in the culture of Uzbekistan."

The next few weeks were a whirlwind of banquets; evenings at the theater and opera; trips to hospitals, children's centers, and factories; and long talks with Eisenstein. "The people have gone mad over [Paul]," Essie wrote home. No less a figure than Maxim Litvinov, the Soviet foreign minister, entertained the Robesons at his home on Christmas Eve. He told Robeson that Russia understood the plight of Black Americans and "were one" with them.

The following week, at dinner with the theater director Alexander Tairov, Robeson was impressed with the wide-ranging talk about African art, music, and culture. His many talks with Eisenstein, too, confirmed the Soviet Union's honorable intentions regarding its "national minorities." The term, Eisenstein explained, had been chosen to replace "primitives," with its unjust implications of inferiority. Eisenstein further explained that Soviet sympathy for minorities could be seen in its "ethnic enclaves," where minority languages and literature were studied in the schools.

Robeson made a point of separately questioning a number of Black Americans who'd chosen to live in the Soviet Union. They expressed their deep contentment with life there and declared it entirely free of racial prejudice. Their testimony was uniformly positive, and Robeson heard no counternarrative to contradict it. It was precisely what he'd *hoped* to hear, but that didn't necessarily mean that the Black community was bearing false witness, under pressure or otherwise.

In the early 1930s the Soviet government's respect for its national minorities did mark a genuine advance over the attitude of the czars—the hereditary, oppressive rulers who'd been overthrown in the communist revolution of 1917. By the late 1930s, with Soviet leader Joseph Stalin in full dictatorial control of the country, the picture would become decidedly more clouded, and one of Essie's brothers would return to the United States disillusioned.

Toward the end of Robeson's two-week stay, Eisenstein screened some of his films. Robeson's favorite was *General Line*, the story of a rural woman who inspires her fellow farmers to form an agricultural cooperative to share land and resources, which he called "easily the finest film I've seen."

The two men also hit it off personally and talked at length about the possibility of working together. Eisenstein had long hoped to make a film about the Haitian revolution, which he'd tentatively titled *Black Majesty* (he had earlier suggested the project to Hollywood's Paramount Pictures—which had swiftly rejected it). Eisenstein also mentioned to Robeson several other possible collaborations, including one based on *Stevedore*, an American play about the struggles of working-class life. Unfortunately Boris Shumyatsky, the head of the Soviet film industry at the time, disliked Eisenstein—perhaps because he was homosexual—and systematically vetoed his projects. (Shumyatsky himself would soon fall out of favor with Stalin and would be executed in 1938.)

Before the Robesons returned to London, Paul told Eisenstein how deeply moved he'd been at his reception, at "the expression of sincere comradeship toward me, as a black man, as a member of one of the most oppressed of human groups." As Paul would later write during the visit, he'd "felt like a human being . . . not a Negro but a human being. . . . Here, for the first time in my life, I walk in full human dignity." This didn't mean that Robeson had become committed to Marxist socialism (the ownership by the state of the means of production and distribution), the economic system of the communist Soviet Union. He even told one reporter that he still considered himself "completely nonpolitical."

Robeson always took his time when making any fundamental decision: his gut feelings and his intellect had to agree. In 1934 he still knew nothing about the dark side of Stalin and the Soviet Union: the forced collectivization of farms, in which millions of peasants had their land, and sometimes their grain, seized and redistributed by the state; the devastating famine in Ukraine; and the accelerating murders of Stalin's political opponents. What he did know was the profound humanitarianism of the revolutionaries who'd originally overthrown the czarist tyranny. And thanks to that day in Berlin, he felt strongly that Nazi fascism was the opposite of Soviet communism. From that time on, the two dueling political philosophies became emotionally linked for Robeson, representing evil and good.

Unlike many left-wing Americans in the 1930s, Robeson did not join the Communist Party, nor would he ever do so. But following his 1934 trip, Robeson did view the Soviet Union as the leading protector against fascism and the champion of minority rights.

Paul's Plan

"Paul is extraordinarily happy these days," Essie wrote her mother early in 1935. He now had a plan: he would earn enough money over the next two years to free himself from financial worry and to allow more time for political activity.

The first step would be a two-month concert tour of England. Then, in small theaters, he would try out two promising plays with political themes. One was *Basalik*, about an African chief who resists white encroachment into his land. The other was *Stevedore*, a play of racial and trade-union conflict that had been successful in New York and had interested Eisenstein. If the two plays were well received, Robeson planned to tour them in regional theaters around England for six months. He hoped that would provide enough income to travel in Africa for a year and then to pay a return visit to the Soviet Union.

Like much of the world, England was in an economic depression at the time. Still, the concert tour drew large crowds everywhere. The two theater ventures proved a good deal less successful. The critics found *Basalik* thin and unsatisfying, and gave no encouragement for extending its run beyond three trial performances. The second play, *Stevedore*, told the story of a Black worker falsely accused of raping a white woman and threatened with lynching by a rampaging mob—which was turned away when white and Black union workers formed a united front against it. The melodramatic, simplistic plot appealed neither to the critics nor to ticket buyers, and Robeson's original plan to tour the two plays fell by the wayside.

Even so, he continued to get a number of promising offers. A prominent director asked him to play the leading role of Mephisto, the Devil, in a film adaptation of Gounod's opera *Faust*. Two other offers, however, held more appeal. The first was to portray Toussaint L'Ouverture, the Haitian liberator, in a play by the radical Trinidadian C.L.R. James, whom Robeson had met in London a few years earlier. The other was to re-create his role as Joe in the film version of *Show Boat*, for forty thousand dollars (roughly equal to half a million dollars today). The Toussaint play would satisfy Robeson's determination to become more active politically, while the *Show Boat* movie would secure his financial needs.

First up was *Show Boat*. In September 1935 Paul and Essie took up residence in a grand flat in Pasadena, outside Los Angeles. Each had a bedroom so that, as Essie put it, "we can all live happily and comfortably, without getting under each other's heels." The two months of filming went well. The relationships on the set were cordial, and Robeson was delighted with the film's gifted director, James Whale, from whom he learned a great deal about how to use his voice to maximum advantage.

Throughout the filming Paul was in marvelous voice and spirits. When the hectic schedule was over, Whale wrote him to say, "Your 'Joe' is really magnificent," and for a time it seemed as if the two would soon work together again. Jerome Kern and Oscar Hammerstein II, the writers of *Show Boat*, had become excited about C.L.R. James's play about Toussaint. They bought the film rights, with Whale their choice for director. For reasons unknown, Hammerstein soon lost interest, and the project was canceled.

But Robeson was still intensely interested in Toussaint's story. In January 1936 he returned to London to do several tryout performances of C.L.R. James's play, but the critics were decidedly lukewarm, and that project also died. Yet the rehearsal period gave James and Robeson the chance to get to know each other better, and for years the two would remain in contact, each deeply admiring the other.

James felt that Robeson's power onstage was due primarily not to his acting ability but to the immensity of his personality. He was a man, as James later put it, "not only of great gentleness but of great command." James also felt that Robeson cared far more for the good he might do in the world than for the glamour or material rewards of a theatrical career. Yet he didn't feel that Robeson, a man of deep reserve, had as yet made any profound political commitment. He was not, in James's opinion, "a revolutionary political person, whose whole life was spent, wherever possible, in striking blows at capitalist society. He was on the side of the revolution, he was on the side of black people, he was on the side of all who were seeking emancipation. But that wasn't his whole life. He was a distinguished person giving himself to revolutionary views."

"The Human Stem"

Robeson, meanwhile, intensified his self-education. He read most of the leading Africanists, people who specialized in African studies or wrote about African people and politics. He filled notebook after notebook with his reactions. As well, he joined Jomo Kenyatta and other future leaders of their countries at gatherings at the West African Students' Union.

In addition, Robeson developed an especially fruitful exchange of views with Norman Leys, a white doctor and committed socialist who'd lived for some fifteen years in East Africa. Leys had written the influential book *Kenya* and had spent a lifetime pleading the African cause in Britain. Leys and Robeson disagreed on some important issues, yet deeply respected each other's integrity and genuine concern for Africa's well-being.

Leys felt that the divisive nature of African tribalism had made it easier for Europeans to exploit the continent, which in turn had depleted its cultural richness. He felt, too, that Africa's best hope lay in modernizing along Western lines. Robeson's views were less settled than those of Leys. In his notebooks for 1936 he debated first with himself—and then with Leys—about whether there was such a thing as "a specifically African philosophy and way of life" and, if so, whether Black Americans were already too culturally "degraded" to identify with it.

Robeson acknowledged that "my own people want to be 100% Americans and deny their possession of racial characteristics," yet at the same time he felt that "emotionally, the modern American Negro would find himself quite at home in Africa, that the bond was one not only of race but of culture—of attitudes to life, a way of living." He believed that "in every black man flows the rhythm of Africa" and that "we can get nowhere until we are proud of being black—and by the same token demand respect of other people of the world. For no one respects a man who does not respect himself."

Leys, on the other hand, rejected the notion that Black people carried with them from their African past some "unique essence," and he argued that no evidence existed to prove that Africans were different because of their special tribal heritage. Because tribal cultures varied greatly, Leys pointed out, there was no solid reason to think that all Africans could unify under one cultural banner. He further pointed out to Robeson that the idea of a special racial character or essence "delighted" racist white people, who could twist it to support their conviction that Black people were genetically inferior.

Robeson insisted that he based nothing "on distinctions of race—they are too vague." *Cultural* differences, though, did exist and could not be avoided. Leys agreed that cultural differences were real, but he went on to argue that no one had the right, in the name of preserving "tradition," to deny an individual or a group exposure to new ideas. Leys found nothing inherently evil in Western scientific thought, certainly not when defined as a process for discovering truth rather than as mere information gathering. "World citizenship," Leys insisted, "means in practice maximizing both liberty and variety *inside* every human group," whether it be a family, a race, or a nation-state.

For Robeson such views were typically Western. They gave primary value to the needs of the individual rather than the community. He agreed with Leys that the option of becoming "world citizens" must be made available to Africans, but he hoped they'd use that opportunity selectively, choosing to incorporate only those aspects of the "new" that would better help them sustain their traditional emphasis on the needs and values of the community as a whole.

Robeson agreed that Western science did increase our power over the *external* world, but in his view the "ultimate questions" lay in the realm of values, not information. African culture, as Robeson saw it, primarily emphasized the inner life and community values. It did not believe, as did many in the West, that wealth was the ultimate goal of human activity. He acknowledged to Leys the irony of his own position. Many Black Americans admired him precisely because he'd accumulated the fame and luxury that they believed were the surest guarantees of happiness. But he did not share their view, feeling instead that "deep down inside me I am African, and for me the African life has a much deeper significance."

Robeson continued to probe and modify his own arguments, not settling for airtight views that rigidly rejected new experiences and insights. He was never a complete socialist or anarchist—or, for that matter, Christian. He once wrote that it was delusional to think "that the way out of bondage lay in deliverance by some act of a God who has been curiously deaf for many centuries; for certainly if prayer and song and supplication could effect a release, the Negro in America would long ago have been free."

By the end of the 1930s, as Robeson became increasingly attracted to an internationalist socialist vision, he became less preoccupied about preserving African culture. His sense of urgency shifted focus from preserving *Black* values to emphasizing the overriding importance of *human* values. One entry in his notebook captures the essence of his ultimate position:

> *I feel certain that all races, all Peoples, are not nearly as different one from the other as textbooks would have it. . . . Most differences are only superficial. The history of mankind proves this. No pure race. No pure culture. No people has lived by itself. . . . The concern of American Negroes should be to make America socialist . . . if the world is to prosper it must be broadened to transcend national boundaries, toward the possible synthesis of, and on the other hand constant interplay between, related cultural forms . . . the human stem is one.*

It's like the branches of a tree, Robeson argued. If the branches are lopped off and set in separate soil, they will die. But attached to a shared trunk and nourished equally, all thrive.

More Movies

During 1936, the busiest year in Robeson's film career, he tried to incorporate his new political values into his artistic life. He recorded a prologue for Joseph Best's *My Song Goes Forth*, a documentary film about South Africa, and made two feature-length

*Paul Robeson leaves London in 1935 on
the first leg of a European tour*

films with African themes. And for the first time he tried to make sure through contract guarantees that he'd be better able than before to have a say in the final products, as he had not with the disappointing *Sanders of the River*.

For *My Song Goes Forth*, Robeson revised the prologue over and over. The final draft included these lines in his narration: "Every foot of Africa is now parceled out among the white races. Why has this happened? . . . If you listen to men like [fascist Italian dictator] Mussolini, they will tell you it is to *civilize*—a divine task, entrusted to the enlightened peoples to carry the torch of light and learning and to benefit the African people. [But in truth] Africa was opened up by the white man for the benefit of himself—to obtain the wealth it contained."

For the first of his new feature films, *Song of Freedom*, Robeson tried to get "final cut" approval written into his contract, but Universal Studios stonewalled him. Nonetheless, he saw appealing possibilities in his role as a London dockworker who discovers that he is descended from a line of African kings, and returns to his people. Robeson was particularly excited about the film's dockside scenes showing Black people coping with the trials and pleasures of ordinary life—a welcome switch from the standard film stereotypes of them as shuffling idiots, faithful servants, happy-go-lucky ne'er-do-wells, or conscience-free gangsters. Robeson felt that he'd been given "a *real* part" for the first time, and later in life he continued to refer to it as one of only two film roles in which he took any pride. (The other was in *Proud Valley*, which he would make several years later.)

After completing *Song of Freedom*, Robeson took a short

A poster for the film Song of Freedom

vacation in Russia, and then, within a few months, he began work on another feature film, *King Solomon's Mines.*

Based on a popular novel by British writer H. Rider Haggard, *King Solomon's Mines* was an elaborate production with a ridiculous plot, packed with thousands of natives clad in "authentic" animal skins. The story line had Umbopa (Robeson), servant to a white man, reveal his true identity as an African king (again!), regain his throne, and save the lives of his treasure-hunting white friends. The narrative was absurd, the musical score wholly inauthentic—and the film overall did nothing to advance Robeson's political views, as he'd initially hoped. The *Pittsburgh Courier*, a Black paper, summed up the generally negative reception: "Robeson is made to sing childish lyrics to dreary tunes in the most unlikely circumstances."

Two more film projects soon followed, but neither fared much better. In the first, *Big Fella*, Robeson once again played a dockworker, a decent, trustworthy fellow—yet one who kept unaccountably bursting into anachronistic song. *Jericho*, the film that followed, was no improvement. Robeson enjoyed the monthlong shoot in Egypt and the company of his co-stars, yet the end result disappointed. Robeson played an army recruit who, once again, ends up being revealed as the beneficent leader of an African tribe (this time of the Tuareg people of North Africa)—and along the way bursts yet again into irrelevant song. The critics were at best lukewarm, and *Jericho* was a box-office failure. Fortunately, Robeson had other, more fulfilling passions that soon found an outlet.

A Song for the Ancient Pharaohs

Although he learned the part of the high priest Sarastro in Mozart's German-language opera *The Magic Flute*, Paul never performed in the full opera (or any other) onstage. A few years after
studying the part, he sang a segment of it in a most unexpected
place—the heart of the Great Pyramid of Egypt.

In 1936 Robeson spent a month in Egypt, filming scenes for
a movie called *Jericho*. The scenes were shot at a site across the
road from the Pyramids, and one day Robeson and two of his co-
stars, with the help of a local guide, worked their way into the
King's Chamber at the center of the ancient stone monument.
They discovered that it had what the actor Henry Wilcoxon called
"the most incredible echo." Wilcoxon suggested that Robeson
should try singing, and the first note, he said, "almost crumbled
the place.... This was Paul Robeson plus!"[3]

Then Robeson started to sing "O Isis und Osiris" from *The
Magic Flute*—a song in which Sarastro asks the gods of ancient
Egypt to protect the hero and heroine. When he'd finished and the
last echo had died away, all four men were in tears. Hardly saying
a word, they left the King's Chamber to its long sleep.

Chapter 7

THE WORLD
GOES TO WAR

FILM WORK CONTRIBUTED TO ROBESON'S FAME AND
helped to pay his bills, but he found far more purpose and satis-
faction in lending his support to various political causes. Early in
1937, for example, he appeared in a concert at a London theater
to aid women made homeless by civil war in Spain—a conflict
Robeson would soon witness firsthand.

He also began to connect himself with the work of the International Committee on African Affairs, an anti-imperialist
organization that was later known as the Council on African
Affairs. It worked to educate people about the connections between the struggle of Black Americans and those of colonized
peoples in Africa and elsewhere. Robeson would become the
chair of the organization in 1941.

Life in Russia

He made several trips to the Soviet Union in 1937. In contrast
to the economically depressed West, Russia, Robeson felt, had

Essie Robeson's mother, known as Ma Goode, and Paul Robeson Jr.

"plenty of food." He made a point of visiting workers' homes and reported that "they all live in healthful surroundings," adding that he wished "the Negroes in Harlem and the South had such places to stay in." Apparently he still saw and heard nothing (or chose to ignore it) about the forced collectivization of Soviet agriculture, the widespread famine, and the loss of millions of lives—with the "national minority" populations in Kazakhstan and Ukraine being especially hard hit.

The Robesons found conditions in Russia so much better than in the United States that they decided early in 1937 to leave Pauli in school there in the care of Essie's mother, Ma Goode. When Paul and Essie returned to Russia that summer, they found the pair "very well," and spent several months soaking up Soviet culture. The highlight was a trip to hear the Uzbek Opera.

Robeson was thrilled that the Uzbeks, a previously oppressed Mongolian people of Central Asia, were being encouraged under the Soviet regime to preserve their cultural identity and also welcomed on equal terms into full citizenship. It confirmed for him that the Soviet constitution's declaration of "the equality of all citizens . . . irrespective of their nationality or race" was in practice a reality. In Robeson's view, this stood in sharp contrast to the policies of most of the contemporary world, where doctrines of "the inferiority of my people are propagated even in the highest schools of learning."

"I Want to Go to Spain"

The Soviet achievement, in Robeson's view, stood in particular contrast to what was happening in Spain. In 1936 Spain's left-leaning government, the Second Spanish Republic, which had socialist and communist elements, had been confronted by a military coup. The country was in the throes of a bloody conflict between the Republicans, loyal to the government, and the Nationalists, a right-leaning coalition led by General Francisco Franco.

Spain was divided, with the Nationalists receiving aid from fascist Italy and Nazi Germany, the Republicans from the Soviet Union and Mexico. Some countries, including the United States, officially supported the Spanish Republic—but with words only. Thousands of Americans and citizens from other countries, however, went to Spain to join the fight, mostly on the side of the Republicans.

To demonstrate his own commitment to the cause, Robeson interrupted his holiday in Russia to give a number of concerts to raise funds in support of the Republicans.

Then, in December 1937, Paul announced to Essie, "I want to go to Spain."

At first she resisted. "Why need he go into the war area, into danger, perhaps risk his life, his voice?" she wrote to friends. But Robeson was determined. "This is our fight, my fight," he told Essie. If need be, he would go alone. Essie knew that when Paul was determined, nothing could stop him from taking a course of action he thought necessary. She ultimately decided to accompany him, and the Robesons crossed over the Spanish border on January 23, 1938. They were warmly welcomed, and a militiaman drove them to Barcelona.

The press turned out to greet them at the Majestic Hotel. Nicolás Guillén, an Afro Cuban writer, vividly described the scene: "Blockaded by a crowd of people hanging on his most insignificant gestures, Robeson pays attention to everyone, smiling. . . . When he talks, he talks passionately."

The views Robeson expressed shifted between moderation and militancy, coming down closer to militancy. As he said, "I belong to an oppressed race, discriminated against, one that could not live if fascism triumphed in the world." His experience in Spain accelerated his commitment to that view. Horrified at what he called the "absolute savagery" of the fascists, he angrily denounced the "so-called democracies" of Britain, France, and the United States for "standing by inactive."

Leaving Madrid, the Robesons drove to Benicasim, to a base hospital near the front lines, where he sang three separate times within a single hour for the wounded, convalescent troops. At their next stops, International Brigades (volunteers who'd come from Britain and the United States to fight on the side of the Republicans) crowded around Robeson with shouted greetings. He was delighted to discover that among the international forces was a sizable group of "the brothers," Black volunteers in the Abraham Lincoln Brigade, which was integrated up to and including command positions.

When the Robeson party moved on to Madrid, they came within range of the fascist artillery; the city was fired on nearly every day. Yet the Robesons went directly to the barracks on the

Robeson singing to Loyalist troops in Spain, 1938

front line. Paul talked and sang with the soldiers, who called out requests to him in various languages.

Everywhere in Madrid, the Robesons were tumultuously welcomed; they met the remarkable communist leader Dolores Ibárruri, called La Pasionaria, and did multiple broadcasts and interviews. When they sat in the audience at a theater, they were recognized, and the cast sang folk songs and danced in Paul's honor. He in turn took to the stage to sing to *them*.

The trip to Spain left a profound impression on Essie as well as Paul. She wrote to a friend that she hadn't been "fundamentally interested" in politics, but now felt that she was rapidly "catching up" with Paul's commitment. As for Paul, he called the 1938 trip to Spain "a major turning point in my life," one that strengthened his already well-developed political

Black American Fighters in Spain

The International Brigades were made up of about 35,000 volunteers from a number of countries who went to Spain to fight alongside the Republicans against the fascist forces that had toppled the left-leaning elected government. Not all members of the brigades were soldiers—most were civilians who felt moved to join the struggle. Approximately three thousand American volunteers served in the Lincoln Brigade and later in the Lincoln-Washington Battalion.

The Lincoln Brigade was racially integrated. One of its most honored members was Oliver Law, a Black labor organizer from Texas who had served for six years in the U.S. Army. He commanded a machine-gun regiment in the Lincoln Brigade and briefly commanded the entire brigade before being killed in combat.

The more Robeson heard about the "quiet, dark brown, strongly built, dignified" Oliver Law, who had kept his men's spirits up by joining in every task he asked of them, the more Robeson was determined to tell his story in film. He envisioned a movie that would center on Law but would also tell the story of what Robeson called "all the American Negro comrades who have come to fight and die for Spain."[6] Like Robeson's vision of an Eisenstein movie or a C.L.R. James play about Toussaint L'Ouverture, such a film would have been an opportunity for Robeson to bring his deeply held values fully into his professional work. Sadly, like those earlier visions, the project of a movie about Oliver Law never got off the ground—for which Robeson blamed the "money interests" controlling the film industry.

sympathies. "I have never met such courage in a people," he told a reporter.

Robeson had always disliked the idea of turning to war to solve problems, but he felt that the Spanish people couldn't simply stand there and "just be murdered." In his notebook he wrote that "Spain is our Front Line," and he deplored the failure of the Western democracies to aid the antifascist cause. In contrast, he noted, the Soviet Union *had* been enthusiastic supporters of the Spanish Republic. As Robeson saw it, the Soviets had proved themselves as standing in the forefront of the struggle for democratic liberties everywhere.

Tragically, within a few months of the Robesons' visit to Spain, Franco's fascists captured Madrid. The remaining members of the International Brigades scattered, and for the next forty years, the Spanish people would live and suffer under a dictatorship.

Heading Toward War

The defeat of republicanism in Spain ran parallel to the rise of Hitler's fascist Third Reich in Germany. Just one generation after the Great War, "the war to end all wars"—now called World War I—the nations of Europe and beyond seemed poised on the brink of another massive conflict.

Germany and its allies had been defeated in World War I by the Allied nations, led by Britain, France, and, eventually, the United States. Now, under Hitler, German anger about the loss of territory and other strict measures imposed by the Allies after that defeat was building toward another war in Europe. In Asia, Japan's attempt to control more of Asia was fueling rivalry with China, where a communist revolution was under way. The mounting conflict would inflame much of the world. For Robeson personally, the war years would bring both one of his greatest acting triumphs and the start of a difficult new stage in his political life.

In the meantime, word had begun to leak out of the Soviet Union about secret "purge" trials that had eliminated large numbers of people whom Stalin considered enemies. Some evidence exists that by the late 1930s Robeson had made some pointed inquiries into the "absence" of certain close friends, but it's unclear how much he knew about Stalin's paranoid and murderous persecution of his so-called "opponents."

As global warfare became ever more likely, Robeson began to mull over the idea of the family returning to the States. He made it clear in press interviews that "something inside had turned," that he was fed up with playing stage and film roles that misused his talent and defamed his people. "I am tired," he told one reporter, "of playing Stepin Fetchit comics and savages with leopard skins and spears." To another, he swore that he would never again do a part like the one in *Sanders of the River*, a film he now called "a total loss."

In the future, he announced, he vowed to appear only "in stories that had some bearing on the problems" ordinary people faced in their daily lives—and at a box-office price they could afford. He felt the same about concert tours: instead of

Stepin Fetchit: A Two-Sided Stereotype

When Paul Robeson declared, "I am tired of playing Stepin Fetchit comics," he was referring to a character created by Lincoln Perry (1902–85), who has been called America's first Black film star.[10] Perry invented Stepin Fetchit ("step and fetch it") to land a role in a 1927 movie called *In Old Kentucky*. His portrayal of the character—a bumbling, fumbling fool billed as "the Laziest Man in the World"—went on to appear in forty-four films by 1939 and made Perry a millionaire.

Perry's career slowed after that, and by the early 1950s, the Stepin Fetchit character had increasingly fallen out of favor with Black Americans, particularly those active in the growing struggle for civil rights. They saw Fetchit as a crude, degrading stereotype built on old slavery-based views of Black people as stupid and incompetent. More recently, though, scholars have pointed out that many Black viewers of Perry's time would have appreciated Fetchit as a version of the enduring "trickster" character, one who cleverly fooled the white people around him by pretending to be useless. In most of Perry's performances, the white people, frustrated because Fetchit appeared unable to follow instructions or do a job, wound up doing the work themselves.

remaining with the prestigious Celebrity Concert series, he started to perform multiple concerts for reduced fees at popular cinema palaces.

Robeson was also determined to lend his name and presence much more frequently to political causes and organizations. In the period just before leaving London to return to the States, he appeared at events to support the Spanish Medical Aid Committee, the Labour and Trade Union Movement, the National Unemployed Workers' Movement, the League for the Boycott of Aggressor Nations, the Coloured Film Artists' Association, and a host of others. He also turned down any number of roles that would have had him repeating yet again some stereotypical version of Black life and culture.

Just a month before the Robesons took Pauli out of school and made the final decision to leave Europe, a wholly unexpected offer came Paul's way. Michael Balcon, head of Ealing Studios, offered him a role that matched his politics: the lead in *Proud Valley*, a fictionalized narrative about the life and plight of the Welsh miners. Their story is told in the film through the eyes of an unemployed American Black man who, through a series of believable accidents, goes to work in the Welsh mines and becomes centrally involved in the miners' struggle for a better life.

Just as shooting for the film began in August 1938, Stalin signed a notorious "nonaggression" pact with Hitler declaring that the Soviet Union and Nazi Germany, the nations that Robeson saw as ideological opposites, would not make war on each other. It was a disillusioning blow to many Soviet supporters. Robeson, though, blamed the unwillingness of the British and French governments to join the Soviet Union in guaranteeing collective security. This left the Soviet Union, he felt, with no way to protect its borders other than by making a deal with Germany.

On September 1, 1939, Hitler's battalions invaded Poland, plunging Europe into war. London swiftly set about mounting antiaircraft guns on building tops, stacking sandbags against windows, and organizing a system of air-raid warnings and blackouts. Each morning Essie drove Paul out to the Ealing studio, and each evening he returned on the Underground, the British subway system. In between he had to fit in both recording sessions and filming. Though the tension and exhaustion took a toll, Robeson's fellow actors on the set of *Proud Valley* found him, as one of them put it, "easy to work with."

Filming was completed on September 25. On September 28 Robeson saw a rough cut of the film and was delighted with it. On September 29 Essie sent off twenty-four pieces of luggage, and the next morning the Robeson family said good-bye to Europe.

Chapter 8

HERO—AND TRAITOR?

BACK IN NEW YORK, PAUL AND ESSIE MOVED INTO the Roger Morris, a fashionable Harlem building, with separate quarters in the penthouse for Essie's mother and Pauli. Within just a few weeks, CBS Radio approached Robeson to perform "Ballad for Americans," and he immediately agreed. The patriotic song was broadcast on November 5, 1939, and created an instant sensation. Robeson repeated the broadcast again on New Year's Day, then recorded the song for Victor Records and watched it climb swiftly to the top of the charts.

Robeson was rapturously hailed as a national hero—yet when, after the second broadcast, he went to meet friends for lunch at the Hotel Elysée, the management informed him that he could eat there only if kept out of sight of its other guests. The star of CBS remained a second-class citizen.

To add to the irony, Hamilton College in New York State soon afterward awarded Robeson an honorary Doctor of Humane Letters degree. He made it a point in his acceptance speech to declare that "the future reorganization of civilization," which so many people were heralding, would need to include elements of African and Asian cultures.

In 1940 Robeson's continued support for the Soviet Union

still raised only minor criticism, and his popularity with the general public remained high. When in May he appeared in a revival of *Show Boat*, the gala opening-night audience greeted his entrance onstage with an ovation.

His concert tour that same year got a marvelous reception in city after city. When he performed "Ballad for Americans" in the Hollywood Bowl, the sold-out crowd was the largest that had ever attended an event there. Another sign of the public's high regard for him was the reception of the movie *Proud Valley* when it opened in New York. Though the film itself got luke-warm reviews, Robeson was praised to the skies. Not a single reviewer brought up what a few rabid conservatives had started to call his "dangerous" tendency to mix politics with art. Those who opposed even modified socialist views were suspicious of anyone who said anything positive about the Soviet Union—and Robeson's high visibility as a successful Black American made his political views even more disturbing to some.

Robeson didn't let criticism keep him from lending his voice and prestige to progressive political groups. He did a radio performance introducing the songs of the International Brigades from the Spanish Civil War, and he helped to dedicate the Children's Aid Society in Harlem. He also appeared at a mass meeting to protest the United States entering the war in Europe, which he saw as essentially designed to protect the profits of the wealthy and to defend the British Empire. Robeson spoke out angrily against the continuing refusal of the British ruling class to give its colonial possessions in India, Ireland, and Africa their freedom. He also lent his support to a biracial trade-union movement, believing that it was the most promising vehicle for extending American democracy to Black workers.

A New Political Landscape

The nonaggression pact between Hitler and Stalin crumbled in June 1941, when Nazi Germany invaded the Soviet Union. The invasion brought about an international realignment. Now, instead of denouncing communism and the Soviet Union, the Western democracies hailed the Soviets—as Robeson had all along—as the front line of defense in the struggle against fascism. Among the Western powers, the former dominant view of the Soviet Union as an aggressive dictatorship gave way to the image of a heroic Russian homeland battling to preserve the integrity of its borders against fascist Nazi aggression.

And with this shift in the Soviet Union's alignment, Robeson, too, made a major adjustment in his position. He went from opposing U.S. intervention in Europe's war to urging President Franklin D. Roosevelt to provide massive aid to the Allies (mainly France, Great Britain, and now the Soviet Union) who were fighting against the Axis (Germany, Italy, and, after the bombing of Pearl Harbor in Hawaii in December 1941, Japan).

The United States joined the war on the side of the Allies in late 1941. With the Soviet Union now a wartime ally, the cause of Soviet war relief became entirely respectable. Robeson participated in massive rallies at Madison Square Garden to raise money for arms for the Soviet people, and a host of mainstream figures seconded his call. *Life* magazine devoted an entire issue to singing the praises of Soviet-American cooperation, and the mainstream magazine *Collier's* inaccurately described the Soviet Union as neither socialist nor communist, but rather "a modified capitalist set-up" moving "toward something resembling our own and Great Britain's democracy." A nationwide poll asking whether the Soviet Union had "as good" a government "as she could have for her people" found only 28 percent saying no.

Not everybody cheered the new international alignment. Right-wing American conservatives continued to believe that the Soviet Union's underlying goal, only temporarily set aside during the war, was to undermine democracy and spread the influence of communism worldwide. J. Edgar Hoover, director of the FBI and feverishly anticommunist, became convinced that Robeson was a Soviet tool and a secret member of the Communist Party of the United States (CPUSA). Robeson was not and never would be a member, yet Hoover assigned special agents to keep close watch on him, convinced that he'd become an active communist agent. This marked the beginning of years of government surveillance and, eventually, harassment of Robeson.

As early as 1942 the FBI was describing Robeson's "activities in behalf of the Communist Party as too numerous to be recorded." FBI agents tapped his phone conversations, bugged his residence, and assigned special agents to trail him daily and file regular reports on his whereabouts.

In April 1943 Hoover placed Robeson on the "custodial detention" list of people who could be immediately arrested in case of national emergency. Yet that very month, Robeson was

Should We Erase a Racist's Name?

J. Edgar Hoover was the director of the Federal Bureau of Investigation from its founding in 1935 to his death in 1972. He oversaw the modernization of the FBI and honed it into a major crime-fighting organization. Yet Hoover is now known to have seriously abused his power.

He also went far beyond what the FBI was legally permitted to do, spying on American citizens who had committed no crimes, keeping secret dossiers of information that could be used to pressure people, and using the FBI to harass left-leaning people like Paul Robeson, whose ideas he hated. Hoover's actions against civil rights leaders and their supporters, including Martin Luther King Jr., were particularly vicious; he also used his power to prevent or delay investigations into crimes by racist groups such as the Ku Klux Klan.

In 1974, the U.S. Congress named a newly built FBI headquarters in Washington, DC, the J. Edgar Hoover Building. In 2015, Representative Steve Cohen of Tennessee introduced a bill to take Hoover's name off the building: "Given his well-documented abuses and prejudices towards African Americans, gays, and lesbians, I believe it is past time to remove his name from this place of honor," Cohen said.[3] The bill failed to pass. Today, in the era of Black Lives Matter and the removal of racist statues from public lands, it might be time to try again.

being hailed in the press for a triumphal concert tour and for starring in a giant Labor for Victory rally in Yankee Stadium.

During the war years, the FBI's secret dossier on Robeson as "a dangerous subversive" and his national popularity grew at the same pace. Ultimately the two would collide, but throughout World War II, the nation's alliance with the Soviet Union coincided with Robeson's own views. This galvanized him into a whirlwind of activity—and considerable acclaim. He crisscrossed the country in a nonstop series of speeches, rallies, and meetings, often interrupting his patriotic pitch to remind the crowd that the nation's wartime mission abroad should be accompanied at home with a determination to end racial discrimination—the goal of which he never lost sight.

In general Robeson's spirits remained buoyant throughout the war, yet he did have moments of discouragement. Now and then he'd confide to a friend that under Roosevelt a certain amount of progress *had* been made in ending discriminatory racial practices, but that the gains thus far remained "pitifully small."

Robeson also became active in the left-wing National Negro Congress. For a time, he served as well as the chair of the Council on African Affairs (CAA), which centered its work on ending colonialism on the continent. Displeased, the FBI promptly labeled the CAA a communist front organization and a leader among groups "presently active in creating considerable unrest among the negroes by stressing racial discrimination"—as if Black Americans needed reminding of race-based inequality.

Far from being cowed, Robeson expanded his organizational commitments. He attended a convention of the left-wing

Southern Negro Youth Congress (SNYC) and then took part in the Southern Conference for Human Welfare. "He was awesome," one person at the SNYC conference reported. "He exuded magnetism and charm and charisma. And he was so gentle and nonegocentric. He had the . . . common touch. You know, you felt you could communicate with him directly. There was no screen. He was available to you."

A Movie Misstep

Being human, Robeson was still capable of errors in judgment. In 1941 he uneasily agreed to act the role of a sharecropper in the Hollywood film *Tales of Manhattan*. He did so thinking the role might be an opportunity to show the plight of the rural Black poor, but when the film was released in 1942, he saw his mistake. The majority of Black reviewers declared, as one of them put it, that it was "difficult to reconcile the Paul Robeson, who has almost single-handedly waged the battle for recognition of the Negro as a true artist, with the . . . simple-minded, docile sharecropper" in *Tales of Manhattan*.

Horrified at the caricature Hollywood had created—"one more plantation hallelujah shouter" is how he described it—Robeson joined the pickets when a demonstration against the film was organized at its opening in Los Angeles. He also called a press conference, at which he announced that he was quitting Hollywood for good.

In truth, Robeson had tried the only options available to a Black performer in those years, and he had found all of them wanting. He'd acted in a race movie in Oscar Micheaux's *Body and Soul*. He'd tried making an experimental art film, *Borderline*, filmed in Switzerland in 1930. And he'd used his limited leverage to change the roles and the scripts offered to him by the major studios. None of these routes had proved satisfying; none had offered him the chance to play parts that represented his sense of political responsibility.

The only solution to big-budget stereotyping, Robeson told the press, was for him to turn to low-budget projects that did not have to make money in the South. He soon found exactly the sort of "alternative cinema" he had in mind: he provided the off-camera narration for Leo Hurwitz and Paul Strand's *Native Land*, a feature-length documentary that reenacted scenes of civil-liberties violations as revealed in testimony before a Senate committee investigating infringements against the Bill of Rights. Robeson accepted the minimal fee *Native Land* could offer—and then made a gift of it to the nonprofit progressive production company Frontier Films.

Making Theater History

Robeson's next venture turned back to the stage—and made history.

Margaret Webster, a noted director of Shakespeare, approached Robeson with the idea of repeating his 1930 London performance in *Othello*, this time on Broadway. She had seen his earlier performance and hadn't thought it very good. Far from being offended, Robeson told her that he agreed with her.

Since then, he added, he'd studied and restudied the role and thought that he now had enough life experience to do more justice to Othello's complex character.

Delighted at his acceptance, Webster approached any number of Broadway theatrical managements and got the same answer from all: Robeson may now feel ready for the role, but the country wasn't. Few Americans would buy tickets to a play in which a Black man made love to, then murdered, a white woman.

Webster turned to summer theater. She accepted an offer from the well-known Brattle Theater in Cambridge, Massachusetts, for a brief tryout run. With Robeson's approval, she made the shrewd decision to offer the roles of Desdemona, the bride, and Iago, the villain, to a married acting pair: Uta Hagen and José Ferrer. Both were rising young stars and both accepted Webster's offer, though Ferrer had never performed Shakespeare and Hagen was still in her early twenties. Against the odds, in a kind of miracle, every element of the production fell into near-perfect place on opening night. The audience erupted into a standing ovation—with the Boston critics adding their praise.

Broadway got the message, and Webster was soon swamped with offers to bring the production to New York. She gave the nod to the prestigious Theatre Guild. Robeson, however, had commitments for a long concert tour and a variety of political appearances, so the transfer to Broadway had to be postponed for a full year. The *Othello* cast finally reassembled for rehearsals in October 1943.

At Robeson's insistence, a full six-week rehearsal period

was scheduled. He thought the Boston critics had overpraised him, and that he needed to dig much more deeply into the role. In particular, he wanted to work on what he viewed as traces of self-consciousness and monotony in his performance. Having grown up in the oratorical tradition of the Black church, he naturally fell back, in moments of doubt, to declaiming a given speech, speaking as though addressing an audience, but this did not always serve his performance well. Robeson always acknowledged—and sometimes exaggerated—the shortcomings of his acting. Uta Hagen later said that "he had a judgment about himself that was astonishing. He didn't fall for praise—other people's accolades never went to his head."

Robeson admired director Margaret Webster, and she worked hard with him on mastering the needed technique to carry off the role of Othello successfully. Yet she wasn't well equipped to help him acquire the particular skills he felt he lacked. She encouraged an external approach that focused on surface effects, shaping the outer form more than probing the inner meaning. Her direction carried the danger of heightening rather than counteracting Robeson's occasional tendency to declaim.

Though the match between director and star wasn't made in heaven, the rehearsal period was marked by warmth and mutual respect. One cast member said that they were "like a family," and another marveled at Robeson's ability to "make everyone feel special." He never shut himself off in a "star's" isolation, to be deferred to, fussed over, and coddled by staff. His easy friendliness included playing on the cast softball team in Central Park and always keeping his dressing-room door open. Nor did he engage in heated political discussions. If asked his opinion, he'd give it, but he made no attempt to overpower others in arguments or to display his political sophistication. "Powerfully cool" is how one cast member sized him up.

When the curtain came down on opening night, *Newsweek* reported, the audience burst "into an ovation that hadn't been heard around those parts in many seasons. For twenty minutes, and half as many curtain calls, the applause and the bravos echoed from orchestra pit and gallery to give Forty-Fourth Street the news of something more than just another hit." The applause finally ended only when Margaret Webster came out onstage and graciously thanked the audience for its enthusiasm.

The daily reviewers agreed that opening night had been "magical" and hailed Robeson for having given a "memorable" and "towering" performance. Theater critics who wrote for weekly papers or magazines mostly saw later performances, and their reviews, though positive, were slightly less glowing. The best known of them, Wolcott Gibbs of the *New Yorker*, definitely gave Robeson his due, praising his "majestic voice," magnificent presence, and "admirably clear" reading of his role. But Gibbs did note that Robeson's movement lacked the natural suppleness of a trained actor.

Years later, Uta Hagen—by then one of the American theater's greatest stars—added her own opinion: what made Robeson a tremendous success as Othello was "his *humanity* onstage . . . everyone melted at his *personality*." Though occasionally he did merely declaim his lines, Hagen added, "the human presence was so big that they went for it anyway."

Minor criticisms mattered little when measured against the

Paul Robeson and Uta Hagen in Othello

significance of Robeson's Othello as a racial event of the first magnitude. As a later Othello, James Earl Jones, put it, the message Robeson conveyed was: "Don't play me cheap. Don't *anybody* play me cheap . . . he reached way beyond arrogance. . . .

Just by his presence, he commanded that nobody play him cheap. And that was astounding to see in 1943."

The Black press, too, saw Robeson's Othello as a milestone in race relations. His old co-star from the film version of *The Emperor Jones*, Fredi Washington, who had become the theatrical editor for a Harlem paper called the *People's Voice*, praised Robeson for having taken "onto the stage his ideals, beliefs and hopes" and for having created "a great social document." She wondered if the powers that be in Hollywood would "become adult enough to shoulder their full democratic responsibilities" and make a *film* of Robeson's Othello. That hope would not be realized. For a decade Robeson had been in demand to portray Black stereotypes on film, but no movie studio ever offered him the chance to play Othello.

But life was not all performing and politics. Throughout the 1940s Robeson was a regular at Café Society, a celebrated club that catered to a mixed-race crowd and was a gathering spot for those with leftist political views. Often accompanied by Uta Hagen, with whom he'd begun an affair, he'd frequently stop for a drink after a performance and listen to the latest singing sensation. Over time Café Society gave significant career boosts to Lena Horne, Zero Mostel, and many other singers, actors, and comedians.

Even at Café Society, however, there were occasional racial incidents. Hagen remembers one night when a drunken white southerner at an adjoining table called out to Robeson, "Your daddy was probably one of my daddy's slaves. You probably belong to me." According to Hagen, "Paul jumped up and started shouting." The manager, who was very fond of him, quickly intervened. It was one of the few times Hagen ever saw Paul "lose his cool."

Othello set an all-time Broadway record for a Shakespearean production with 296 performances. Then, after the show closed on Broadway, the company set out in September 1944 on a thirty-six-week, coast-to-coast tour.

Paul and Uta would stay together for two years. Essie took up residence in Enfield, Connecticut, in a house the Robesons had bought (though Paul was there infrequently). She became active in local politics and also spent considerable time working to become a successful writer. Paul often complained about Essie to Uta, mocking what he saw as her pretentions. Yet lingering affection, interwoven with dependency, remained between the couple, and they would live and travel together again in the years ahead.

Chapter 9

AT THE PEAK OF FAME

IN THE CLOSING DAYS OF WORLD WAR II, ROBESON continued to feel that "the forces of progress are winning." He believed that segregation was under challenge in the United States, that the days of colonialism around the world were drawing to a close, and that the nations of the world would soon fully accept the legitimacy of the Soviet Union. Yet within months of Harry Truman becoming president in April 1945, Robeson's optimism began to fade and his mood began to darken. The end of the war in September did not restore his faith.

Robeson had hoped that the United States would lead the way in proposing that all colonial possessions—not merely those of the defeated Axis powers—be placed under the trusteeship of the United Nations as a step toward complete independence. Yet although the United States did make such a proposal at a United Nations conference in San Francisco in the spring of 1945, it was not what Robeson had hoped for.

The proposal set no limit on how much time would pass before former colonial territories could become independent. It did not require the Allied powers to put their own territorial possessions on the path to independence. Finally, it did not provide for colonial peoples themselves—or the Soviet Union—to be represented on the United Nations' Trusteeship Council, which oversaw the administration of such territories. In fact, within months of the San Francisco meeting, U.S. naval authorities called for greater U.S. control over strategic Pacific islands. Rather than putting an end to the era of imperialism, the Western powers seemed bent on giving it new life.

As for ending racism, Truman appointed several southern segregationists to his cabinet, seeming to signal a determination to defend and maintain racial barriers. In 1946, on their longest ever cross-country concert tour, Robeson and Larry Brown saw deteriorating conditions and dwindling opportunities for people of color everywhere they went.

Between June 1945 and September 1946, fifty-six Black Americans were killed in the United States. The death toll included a particularly brutal lynching in Monroe, Georgia, and a white police riot against Black citizens in Columbia, Tennessee. Much of the violence seemed aimed at "uppity" Black veterans who returned from the front lines of the so-called "struggle for democracy" and dared to act as if the democratic principle applied at home as well. At a protest rally at Madison Square Garden on September 12, 1946, Robeson angrily drew a connection between the "bestial brutality" of the German Nazis and the American Ku Klux Klan.

Two weeks later, following a protest march against lynching in the nation's capital, Robeson led a seven-person delegation to the White House to seek President Truman's support for an antilynching bill. Robeson had barely finished reading aloud the first paragraph of the delegation's statement when Truman irritably interrupted. He was concerned about lynching, he told the group, but the time was not right to try to pass a federal antilynching bill. Though Truman didn't say so, Robeson felt that his refusal to support such a bill was based on the fear that white southerners would desert his Democratic Party in droves.

Truman, raising his voice, reminded the delegation that the United States and Great Britain represented "the last refuge of freedom in the world." Robeson immediately took issue with the president. The British Empire, he said, was "one of the greatest *enslavers* of human beings," one example being its refusal to grant independence to India. Robeson reminded Truman that the temper of Black people had changed, that if the federal government refused to defend its Black citizens against murder, then they would have to defend themselves. Furious, Truman ended the meeting.

The Questions Begin

Within two weeks, Robeson was called to testify before California's Joint Fact-Finding Committee on Un-American Activities, made up of members of the state legislature to uncover so-called communist threats. Such hearings and investigations would soon became common on the state and federal level as the Cold War between the United States and the Soviet Union deepened, and anticommunist fervor grew ever more dominant in American life. Most of the hearings and investigations had little or nothing to do with any actual or suspected crimes. They tried to censor free expression, and they fed a climate of fear in which people were encouraged to "inform" on their friends and colleagues—anyone suspected of having the slightest sympathy for the Soviet Union.

Asked on the stand if he was a member of the Communist Party, Robeson replied that the committee might just as well ask if he was a registered Republican or Democrat; the Communist Party was no less legal. In fact, Robeson continued, he was *not* a member of the party, but he had no reason to believe that communism was "evil"—since communists "were the first people who understood the struggle against fascism and the first to die in it."

The committee members were polite, though unpersuaded. In 1946 Robeson was still a commanding, widely respected figure. Over the next ten years, the politeness would fade, Robeson would be publicly accused of disloyalty to the country, and he would be openly denounced for his support of the Soviet Union.

But in 1947, rather than retreat, Robeson became more politically active than ever. As the United States and Great Britain accelerated their "get tough with Russia" policy, a new political party emerged on the scene in the States. It was the Progressive Party, spearheaded by Truman's secretary of commerce, Henry A. Wallace, and designed to counteract the country's right-wing trend. Central to the Progressive message was the view that nations with different economic systems could, and must, live in peace together. In response, Truman asked for Wallace's resignation from the cabinet, and received it. Robeson joined the Progressive Party early on, though his own political agenda remained focused on combating racism.

When Robeson and Larry Brown reached Peoria, Illinois, on their concert tour, they ran straight into a protest campaign.

The Peoria city council had recently passed a resolution against the appearance of "any speaker or artist who is an avowed propagandist for Un-American ideology," meaning socialism or communism. The city's mayor initially agreed to let the concert take place, but under a barrage of pressure from "patriot" groups, he withdrew the offer "to prevent bloodshed." The local radio station refused to give Robeson airtime to explain his views.

In the end, Robeson had to settle for meeting with a handful of people in the living room of a Black union official. Interviewed by the local press, he declared, "I have been all over the world and the only time I have seen hysteria reach these heights was in Spain under Franco and Germany under Hitler."

The hysteria was just beginning. From that point on Robeson was almost invariably asked the same question wherever he went: "Are you or are you not a member of the Communist Party?" Over and over again, he answered with a variation of the same formula: "There are only two groups in the world today—fascists and antifascists. The communists belong to the antifascist group, and I label myself an antifascist." Though Robeson never joined the Communist Party, true to his principles he would never deny its right to exist. As he told one newspaper reporter, "If Communism means pointing out to the people that their lives are being dominated by a handful, I guess I'm a Communist."

As the Progressive Party prepared to run Henry A. Wallace for the presidency, harassment of leftists mounted in intensity. Throughout 1947, however, Robeson remained a popular public figure. In a Gallup poll released in June, he was named one of forty-eight runners-up in a survey of the public's "ten favorite

Paul Robeson singing at a testimonial dinner in honor of Japanese American World War II veterans, organized by presidential candidate Henry Wallace

people." That same month he sang to a full house at Symphony Hall in Boston, and in July he sold out a large stadium in New York City. Dozens of left-wing organizations continued to vie for his presence at their events, knowing it would guarantee a big turnout. And he did appear at many of them, giving preference to the Civil Rights Congress, the Joint Anti-Fascist Refugee Committee, and the Progressive Party.

Progressives and Problems

At the end of 1947 Wallace formally declared his candidacy for the presidency. Robeson immediately announced his support and became one of five co-chairs of a national Wallace for President committee. There was some movement to nominate Robeson as the vice presidential candidate, but he immediately withdrew his name. Yet throughout 1948 he devoted himself to the Progressives, appearing at rallies in every section of the country. Essie, too, became active in the Progressive ranks. Despite feeling ill from colitis much of the time, she managed to campaign widely on the East Coast.

Many Black Americans were excited about the Wallace movement. The Progressives, after all, had nominated a far larger share of Black candidates than the Republicans or Democrats, and for a wider variety of offices. Everywhere Wallace and Robeson went during the campaign, they called repeatedly for equal rights for Black Americans. Daringly, they even carried that message into the South.

Wallace refused to speak before segregated audiences and defied local Jim Crow ordinances, which led to cross burnings and egg splatterings at his rallies. Robeson, too—despite warnings about his physical safety—campaigned in the Deep South, and in his speeches emphasized the struggle for desegregation, not a defense of the Soviet Union. Ignoring his own danger, Robeson instead highlighted the courage of local Black people who attended his events and sometimes formed protective cordons around him to provide a sense of safety.

President Harry Truman was a cagey opponent. His 1948 reelection campaign strove to identify Henry Wallace in the public mind with communism—even though the Progressive Party was neither inspired nor run by communists. The Truman campaign also counted on Cold War tension with the Soviet Union to make the public fearful that if it "changed horses in mid-stream" and voted for anyone but Truman, procommunist forces would take over the country.

The Communist Party USA (CPUSA) actually helped Truman, in a way, by formally declaring its support for Wallace. Because the CPUSA was a legal party, Wallace—honorably, it could be argued—refused to reject the party's support, though he did make it clear that he was neither a communist nor a socialist.

International developments also weakened Wallace's position. The Progressives argued that American, not Soviet, combativeness had started the Cold War. But that argument lost force when the Soviets backed a totalitarian coup against a democratic government in what is now the Czech Republic, and blockaded the city of Berlin. Soviet policy went a long way toward disproving Henry Wallace's claim that two different economic systems could live side by side in peace.

Truman also directly courted the Black vote. He issued executive orders that desegregated the armed forces and created a Fair Employment Practices Committee—and he shrewdly announced them during a speech in Harlem. In reality, Truman was at best a lukewarm supporter of civil rights, and after the election, he would cut back on his promises. At the time, though, his speech in Harlem successfully wooed many Black voters who'd initially backed Wallace and the Progressives. Among those who shifted their support to Truman and the Democrats were Walter White, head of the NAACP, and Lester Granger, head of the Urban League.

Robeson vs. the Senators

In the midst of these developments, the U.S. Senate Judiciary Committee held hearings on a bill that would require all communist and "communist front" organizations to register. The Progressive Party took the lead in denouncing the bill as an effort "to frighten all the American people into conformity or silence." It insisted that existing laws against treason and sabotage were sufficient protection from any potential danger—unless, as Henry Wallace put it, the country was intent on becoming "a police state."

Both Wallace and Robeson were called to testify before the Senate committee. Wallace, referring to Hitler's campaign against the communists, warned that "the suppression of the constitutional rights of Communists is but the prelude to an attack upon the liberties of all the people." When Robeson took the stand, he was no less forceful. When asked to define what the American communists stood for, Robeson shot back, "For complete equality of the Negro people." When asked for the umpteenth time whether he was a member of the party, Robeson refused to settle for a simple, accurate "no." He replied that the question "has become the very basis of the struggle for American civil liberties." It represented an invasion of the constitutional right to a secret ballot.

The senators weren't pleased. They proceeded to grill Robeson further. Wasn't it true, one of them asked, that American communists owed primary allegiance to the Soviet Union? "I don't think they do have as much allegiance to Russia," he responded, "as certain Americans seem to have today, say, to fascist Greece or to Turkey." And what did he mean by "fascist"? another senator asked. Two things, Robeson answered: "a belief in racial superiority and a monopoly of resources in the hands of a few."

After the hearing, when reporters questioned the senators about the committee meeting, one of them said that "Robeson seems to want to be made a martyr. Maybe we ought to make him one."

Robeson's response was to return to the campaign trail.

As the election approached, the FBI raided the national headquarters of the CPUSA and charged a dozen of its leaders with "advocating forcible overthrow of the government." They were charged under the Smith Act, which had been passed in 1940 and had already been used to fingerprint and register millions and to arrest and convict socialist and communist leaders. Robeson and others publicly warned that the roundup reminded them all too much of the first step fascist governments always take before moving to destroy the democratic rights of all minority groups. Few Black leaders, however, endorsed his statement.

By late summer of 1948, the "lesser of two evils" view had

The Smith Act and the
First Amendment

The Smith Act—more formally called the Alien Registration Act—
had become law in 1940, before the United States entered World
War II but with the prospect of war on the minds of America's
leaders. The act had three main provisions. One required any
adult living in the country who was not a U.S. citizen to register
with the government. Another outlined conditions in which an
alien, or noncitizen, could be deported. The third was aimed at
sedition, which is speech or action that encourages revolt against
the government. It established criminal penalties for anyone, citizen or not, who called for the overthrow of the U.S. government
"by force or violence" or who organized, promoted, or taught any
doctrine that might have such a purpose.

The act had been crafted specifically to give the government a
reason to deport Harry Bridges, a radical labor organizer who had
been born in Australia. But like other antisedition laws before it,
the Smith Act was applied very broadly to suppress statements
and organizations of which the U.S. government disapproved.
More than two hundred people—ranging across the political
spectrum from communists to fascists, but mostly communists—
were charged under the act between 1940 and 1957. At that time
the Supreme Court reversed some of the convictions under the
act, declaring them unconstitutional because they had violated
the First Amendment right to free speech.

come to hold sway with many liberals, Black and white. They feared that support for the Progressive Party would draw enough voters from Truman to elect the Republican candidate, Thomas Dewey, a conservative "law and order" man. In this view, Truman was a lesser evil than Dewey, while Wallace was a lost cause.

While awaiting returns on election night, Robeson sang to the hundreds of campaign workers and supporters who'd gathered at Progressive Party headquarters in New York. The vote proved even more disheartening than expected. While Americans cast more than 24 million votes for Truman, Wallace received just over a million—fewer than J. Strom Thurmond, the candidate of the racist Dixiecrats, who had left the Democratic Party over its threat to extend civil rights to Black people.

The victorious Truman and the Democratic Party viewed his success as support for a "get tough" policy toward communism, both at home and abroad. Truman wasted no time. By early 1949 employees in government service were required to take a "loyalty oath."

Nor did Paul Robeson escape renewed scrutiny. On January 17, 1949, J. Edgar Hoover specifically requested that the New York FBI office update its files on Robeson. Hoover insisted on "a new report . . . setting forth the extent of the subject's present activities in connection with the Communist Party and related groups." Paul Robeson had moved into the crosshairs of Hoover's FBI.

Chapter 10

"THE STRUGGLE" HITS HOME

AFTER THE FAILURE OF THE PROGRESSIVE CAM-paign, Robeson maintained his political activity on all fronts, giving not an inch to those determined to hound him. He even appeared at the New York courthouse where eleven leaders of the Communist Party were about to stand trial on Smith Act charges. As he shook hands with each of the defendants, he said, "I, too, am on trial"—not as a member of the Communist Party, but as a private citizen who cared about civil liberties.

The trial began on March 7, 1949, and would prove to be the most significant legal battle of the Cold War. At the time, Robeson was in Europe on a long concert tour, but he publicly announced that he would return to testify at the trial whenever needed.

The European tour was a replacement for eighty-five concert dates in the United States that had been canceled. At first, Robeson's booking agents had had no trouble arranging the engagements at top fees. Then, when leftist filmmakers later known as the Hollywood Ten were charged, the uproar about communists in the entertainment field made the industry take

*Paul Robeson protesting the Jim Crow segregation policy
at Ford's Theater in Baltimore, Maryland, which eventually
ended its segregation practices a few years later*

a quick dive to the right. Agents in the concert locations caved in and canceled all of Robeson's bookings. It was an ominous sign of how quickly the country was buying into the notion of a communist threat to America's well-being.

But in Europe Robeson's popularity had not diminished. His concerts were sold out, and the tour became something like a four-month triumphal procession. Yet, for the first time in his memory, Robeson became homesick. As he put it, the notion had "never even occurred" to him that "such a thing was possible." He thought his longing to be back in the States came from two causes. One was "the Struggle [against the country's lurch to the right]—my being so much a part of it—it is the most

Banned in South Africa

During the British segment of Robeson's concert tour, he made a number of political appearances. Probably the most noteworthy was his speech at a London conference called to protest the policies of D.F. Malan, the recently elected prime minister of South Africa, a nation in which a white minority of European descent held vastly more power and property than the native African majority of the population. Malan's government had begun to lay the foundations of apartheid—racial separation by law—throughout the country.

Robeson was one of those who spoke out against it.

An East African student who was studying in London at the time recorded the effect one of Robeson's antiapartheid speeches had on him: "The great voice was low and soft but with the suggestion of enormous power behind it. . . . This was no trickster; all that he said was carefully reasoned. . . . There was forcefulness but no arrogance. Instead, there was humility, combined with a deep pride in his race. But he did not confine himself to the struggle of his own race for freedom. He . . . has got beyond mere racialism. He described white people of English descent he had seen living in appalling conditions in America. In many parts of the world there were [Fascistic pockets], whatever name they might be called by locally, and he said it was his business and the business of freedom-loving people everywhere to combat them."[1]

Robeson's words were heard by others as well. Immediately after his speech, the South African government announced a ban on the playing of Paul Robeson's records on the radio throughout the country.

important in the world today, I'm sure of that." The second "has something do with people who have become very dear to me."

He wrote those words to Helen Rosen, a woman he'd met through their mutual involvement in progressive politics. She was a fifth-generation white New Yorker of the van Dernoot family, whom Paul would teasingly call "Miss van der Snoot." She and her husband, Sam, would be devoted to Robeson for the rest of his life, and Helen would become his lover and one of the few people he fully trusted. Indeed, she would become the emotional center of his life.

The Turning Point

In April 1949 Robeson went to Paris to speak at the World Peace Congress. This fateful event, more than anything else, would mark out the path of the last third of his life.

In 1949 tensions and suspicions were running high on both sides of the Cold War. China was about to come under the control of its Communist Party, and in the United States, the rabidly anticommunist conservative right wing was consolidating its influence. The Western powers, on their part, were forming the North Atlantic Treaty Organization (NATO), a mutual defense pact that the Soviets denounced as a sign that capitalist nations had embarked on a new war to push back the advance of socialism.

Two thousand delegates from fifty nations gathered in Paris for the World Peace Congress. W.E.B. DuBois headed the American delegation. Other celebrated figures in attendance

Paul Robeson and W.E.B. DuBois at the
World Peace Congress in Paris, 1949

included the Spanish painter Pablo Picasso, the French poet Louis Aragon, the Nobel laureate in physics Frederic Joliot-Curie; and Pietro Nenni, the newly elected head of the Italian Socialist Party. By the time Robeson stepped up to the podium to speak, the British left-wing politician Konni Zilliacus had already received thunderous applause when he told the delegates that "the workers of Britain will not fight or be dragged into fighting against the Soviet Union."

In his own speech to the delegates, Robeson declared that the wealth of America had been built "on the backs of the white workers from Europe and on the backs of millions of blacks. . . . And we are resolved to share it equally among our children." He ended with words that closely echoed those of Zilliacus, saying that "we shall not put up with any hysterical raving that urges us to make war on anyone. Our will to fight for peace is strong. We shall not make war on anyone. We shall not make war on the Soviet Union."

An American Associated Press reporter in the audience immediately sent off a report that was quickly reprinted across the United States. Unfortunately, the AP dispatch distorted Robeson's words. It claimed that he'd said, "We colonial peoples . . . denounce the policy of the United States government, which is similar to that of Hitler and Goebbels. . . . It is unthinkable that American Negroes would go to war on behalf of those who have oppressed us for generations against a country [the Soviet Union] which in one generation has raised our people to the full dignity of mankind."

Today, misleading or even falsified statements travel around the world at cyberspeed, sometimes destroying reputations and lives in the process. Even in the age of telegraph and newsprint, though, the AP's distorted rendering of Robeson's words produced an immediate uproar that had a lasting, corrosive effect on Robeson's public image. Even if Robeson *had* said the offending words assigned to him, he would not have been the first prominent American to ask angrily whether Black people should fight in the country's foreign wars. During World War II, the courtly, highly respected A. Philip Randolph, head of the Brotherhood of Sleeping Car Porters, had said in an editorial in his newspaper *Messenger*, "No intelligent Negro is willing to lay down his life for the United States as it presently exists."

But when Robeson spoke nearly the same words, he was already (unlike Randolph) under suspicion for "disloyalty." The white press pounced on him. A number of Black leaders, in turn, hurried to say that he did not speak for anyone but himself. And U.S. governmental agencies exchanged furious memos speculating about possible grounds for denying Robeson his citizenship. Robeson had clearly crossed a dangerous line.

For years, Paul Robeson had appeared to white America to be living proof that a "deserving" Black man could make it in the United States. During the Roosevelt presidency, Robeson himself had spoken enthusiastically about America's democratic promise. But in the four years since Roosevelt's death, Robeson's optimism about the country making good on its paper promises had steadily eroded. His increasingly disenchanted public remarks had disturbed the white power structure.

For most of his career, Robeson had filled the role of "showcase Black American." Now, however, he refused any longer to play the "good darkie," failed to stay in line. The powers that be decided that the time had come to isolate and discredit him.

The right-wing press led the charge. One such paper announced that from now on, Robeson "may be dismissed and forgotten." That much came as no surprise. More unexpected was the way *Black* leaders distanced themselves from Robeson. They'd long believed that the best hope for even a modest civil rights program depended on persuading the white power structure that Black people were deferential and patriotic Americans. The white ruling class did not expect, and would not tolerate, anything like militant demands or belligerent behavior. Black Americans were expected to politely ask for their rights, not demand them.

Black people were also expected to isolate any renegade in their midst. The State Department "requested" that Walter

White, head of the NAACP, issue a statement distancing the organization from Robeson. White initially gave a clear and rather bold signal that Robeson was not alone in some of his views. "Many Negroes," White wrote, "will be glad Robeson spoke as he did if it causes white Americans to wake up to the determination of Negroes to break the shackles which race prejudice fastens upon them." But then White fell into line. "Negroes are Americans," his statement for the NAACP emphasized. "In event of any conflict that our nation has with any other nation we will regard ourselves as Americans, and meet the responsibilities imposed on all Americans."

"The Robeson Problem"

Roy Wilkins, who would later head the NAACP and who was profoundly antagonistic to Robeson, asked A. Philip Randolph to call a secret meeting of Black leaders to deal with "the Robeson problem."

Unlike the conservative Wilkins, Randolph was, like Robeson, not a polite petitioner for his rights. He had threatened to call for a Black boycott of the armed services during the Korean War, which was just beginning, unless President Truman issued an executive order dismantling segregation. But Randolph did not share Robeson's admiration for the Soviet Union. Nor did he think it wise for Robeson to have made his radical speech at a conference on foreign soil. As he put it, "There's a sort of unwritten law that if you want to criticize the United States you do it at home. . . . We have to prove that we're patriotic."

Bayard Rustin, Randolph's chief lieutenant, resented the fact that Robeson had spoken as if he were a political leader when, as Rustin put it, he'd never taken "any organizational responsibility for what was happening in the black community. . . . Here is a man who is making some other country [the Soviet Union] better than ours, and we've got to sit here and take the gaff, while he is important enough to traipse all over the country, to be lionized by all these white people, saying things for which he will not take any responsibility." What Rustin ignored was that artists like Robeson are often political, but almost never take on the tedious day-to-day chores of running an organization. In addition, over the previous few years a significant number of white people had stopped "lionizing" Robeson and had begun to view him as a misguided rebel.

Rustin set up a meeting of Black leaders: the civil rights establishment. Twenty were invited, and most of them showed up, including Randolph and Wilkins. At the heart of the agenda, as Rustin later explained it, was to create "a united front to make sure that America understood that the current black leadership totally disagreed with Robeson."

Each leader at the gathering returned to his or her organization and issued a statement about Robeson. Mary McLeod Bethune, president of the National Council of Negro Women, told the press that "American Negroes have always been loyal to America, [and] they always will be; Robeson does not speak for the National Council." Adam Clayton Powell Jr., a congressman and pastor of the influential Abyssinian Baptist Church, had a statement read at all church services declaring that "by no stretch of the imagination can Robeson speak for all Negro people."

Charles H. Houston, chair of the NAACP legal staff, announced that "we would fight any enemy of this country," and Edgar G. Brown, director of the National Negro Council, told its members that Robeson's speech was "pure Communist propaganda."

And so it went, with the leaders of every major Black organization stepping forward—without waiting to learn whether Robeson had been accurately quoted in Paris—to declare their loyalty to the nation and to cast out the disgraced son. Yet what the Black establishment felt it had to do publicly did not necessarily correspond to what some thought privately. Even Bayard Rustin admitted that by staking out a radical position, Robeson had made it more likely that the white power structure would open their ears to more moderate Black leaders who were "only" calling for desegregation.

Speaking Up in Support

The views of the Black establishment didn't necessarily represent the majority of "ordinary" Black citizens; they knew that conservative white people would link any demand for Black equality with "communist subversion." Quite simply, a significant number of Black people shared Robeson's views. As one Black newspaper in North Carolina put it, "There is hardly a Negro living in the South who, at some time or another, has not felt as Robeson expressed himself as being unwilling to lay down his life for a country that insults, lynches and restricts him to second-class citizenship, whether it be in a war against Russia, Germany or Great Britain."

Another Black editorial declared that "a person does not have to be a Communist . . . or echo the Communist line in order to be conscious of the thousands of indignities suffered daily by Negroes." Robeson had never claimed to speak for all Black people, but as the Black press made clear, he clearly did speak for some of them—perhaps for as many as the Black national organizations did. Columnist Abner Berry argued that the heads of the NAACP and other organizations did not have the right to claim in their "breast-beating declarations of patriotism" that they spoke for 15 million Black Americans.

One Black technical sergeant put it more personally in a letter to the *New York Age*. He said that, writing "as a vet who put in nearly five years in our Jim Crow Army, I say Paul Robeson speaks more for the real colored people than the Walter Whites and Adam Powells. . . . I saw the U.S. bring democracy to Italy: white officers kept informing the Italians that the [Black] 92nd Infantry men were rapists and apes."

But it was probably the shrewd, outspoken W.E.B. DuBois, the undisputed patriarch of Black America, who made the most provocative analysis of the 1949 controversy: "I agree with Paul Robeson absolutely that Negroes should never willingly fight in an unjust war. I do not share his honest hope that all will not. A certain sheep-like disposition, inevitably born of slavery, will, I am afraid, lead many of them to join America in any enterprise, provided the whites will grant them equal rights to do wrong."

On the anti-Robeson side of the debate, the lowest blow was struck by a venomous editorial in the May 1949 issue of *The Crisis*, the official organ of the NAACP. The editorial was unsigned, but the author was later revealed to have been Roy

Wilkins. He insisted—contrary to the evidence—that Robeson spoke only "for himself" and that his lack of "service to his race" hardly entitled him even to a personal opinion. The editorial claimed that Robeson had concentrated most of his life on making money and on keeping his fellow Black people at "a safe distance." Wilkins had sunk to a new low in malicious slander.

Yet many Black people remembered that it had been the NAACP that had praised Harry Truman in the recent presidential election. Unlike Robeson, the NAACP had refused to endorse the Progressive Party, though its platform had included a strong call for Black civil rights.

In an outrage-filled letter to the NAACP, the influential Black lawyer and publisher Charles P. Howard accused it of "no longer best serving the people whom it was organized to serve." Instead, Howard said, the NAACP had been "side-tracked into serving the very interests it was organized to fight." Howard reminded the NAACP that "Paul Robeson is recognized by the great masses of the Negro people as more nearly their ideal leader than all of the Walter Whites and Roy Wilkinses in the country and he doesn't get a dime for doing it, only the kicks of Negroes who ought to be appreciating him."

Several other Black leaders spoke up in Robeson's behalf, including the prominent activist Mary Church Terrell, who told Wilkins that she held Robeson "in the highest esteem." She denounced the NAACP's attempt to "belittle" his sacrifice and contribution. The *New York Times* joined the fray with an editorial that probably echoed a view widely held among *white* readers: Robeson was "mistaken and misled." The editorial patronizingly suggested that he give up "making speeches" and return to using "his great gifts" as a concert artist.

Grim Discoveries in Russia

Following the Paris speech that set off the uproar, Robeson remained in Europe for several months to fulfill various concert engagements, including several in Eastern Europe. The tour ended in Moscow, where Robeson was received again with great acclaim. The Moscow press brimmed over with adoring reviews and interviews.

Yet on this trip Robeson felt notably more uneasy. The Soviet Union was in the middle of a notorious "anti-Zionist" campaign falsely claiming that Zionism—support for a Jewish homeland—was a form of racism and similar to Nazi fascism. In reality, the campaign was an attack on Soviet Jewry. Robeson had long been friendly with a number of prominent Russian Jews and in 1943 had hosted two of the most highly regarded when they visited New York: the actor-director Solomon Mikhoels and the writer Itzik Feffer.

Now, six years later in Moscow, Robeson was unable to locate them.

He finally learned that Mikhoels had been murdered by the Soviet secret police. Other well-known Jewish cultural figures were also under arrest. Robeson persisted in asking why he'd been unable to locate his old friend Feffer. Finally, on the eve of

Robeson's departure, Feffer was brought to his hotel. Through mute gestures, Feffer let him know that the room was bugged. The two men kept their talk on the level of superficial pleasantries, while communicating essential facts through a few written notes and gestures. At one point Feffer drew his finger across his throat to signify that he expected to be executed.

Robeson got the message. He decided to end his last concert in Moscow with a direct reference to Feffer. Asking the audience for quiet, he announced that he would sing only a single encore. He then spoke with emotion of the sense he had of the deep cultural ties between the Jewish peoples of the United States and the Soviet Union, a tradition that continued in the present generation of Russian Jewish writers and actors. He spoke, too, of his recent meeting with Itzik Feffer. Then he moved to his one encore: "Zog Nit Kaynmal," the song that had been sung by the resistance movement against the Nazis in the Jewish ghetto of Warsaw, Poland. Robeson recited the words in Russian before singing them in Polish. Here is, in part, an English translation:

Never say that you have reached the very end,
When leaden skies a bitter future may portend,
For sure the hour for which we yearn will yet arrive,
And our marching steps will thunder: we survive!

After a few moments of hushed silence, the dam broke. In a burst of emotion, people rushed the stage, tears in their eyes, shouting their thanks to Robeson and attempting to embrace him.

Robeson apparently felt that if he'd made a more formal

protest to the Soviet authorities about the anti-Semitism campaign, it might have the reverse effect and seal Feffer's fate. Besides, questioning Soviet policy publicly would confirm the right-wing American view that the Soviet Union had become a murderous tyranny. In truth, it *had* become a murderous tyranny, though the full extent of Stalin's reign of terror would not be publicly confirmed until 1956. Neither then nor later did Robeson ever say a word—not to Essie, not to Pauli, not even to Helen Rosen—about how much he already knew about the earlier Soviet purges: the so-called "show trials" in the 1930s that led to the deaths of hundreds if not thousands of Stalin's "enemies."

On returning to the United States soon after his 1949 Moscow concert, Robeson denied to the gaggle of reporters who met his plane that the rumors of anything like an anti-Semitic campaign was under way in the Soviet Union. "I met Jewish people all over the place," he told the reporters. "I heard no word about it." Why? Why even as late as 1949 did Robeson fail to speak out about how Stalin had perverted the original promise of the Russian Revolution and turned his country into a homicidal dictatorship?

How can we begin to understand how a man of Robeson's deep humanity could decide to keep silent when he saw that a once-idealistic revolution, in which millions had invested their hopes and dreams, had been grotesquely turned into something closer to a gangster cartel?

Although Robeson never explained or modified his silence on the tragedy of Stalin's Russia, the answer likely lies in his own ideals and goals.

Faithful to His Ideals

Where politics was concerned, Robeson was first and foremost "a race man." Improving the lot of his own people had always been at the center of his agenda.

During the early 1930s, when Robeson first had direct contact with the Soviet Union, many Western intellectuals and artists had openly expressed their admiration for the Soviet "experiment." They placed their hopes for a better world in its success.

What Robeson had seen on his early trips to the Soviet Union in the 1930s was a set of leaders who—unlike the tyrannical czars who'd been indifferent to the desperate poverty and misery of the Russian masses—promised to give primary attention to improving their lives. Robeson had been thrilled above all that the revolution placed high value on securing the cultural integrity of the Soviet Union's ethnic minorities, even as it offered them all the rights of full citizenship.

As late as 1949 Robeson believed that the Soviets "had done everything" for their national minorities. When he attended the Kazakh Art Festival that year, he came away feeling that it was "a tremendous thing that these people could be there with their literature, music, theater—not after a thousand years, but in hardly one generation." There were those who said that the Soviets "had no black problem because they had no blacks"—to which Robeson answered, "There are of course tens of millions of dark peoples there who would be vigorously Jim Crowed in the United States. Take the people of [Soviet] Georgia. In Tiflis [the Georgian capital], they are very dark, like the Puerto Ricans and Mexicans; and there are millions of yellow people—I have seen how the Chinese are treated in San Francisco."

In the 1930s Robeson had come to believe passionately—and with reason—that American racism and colonialism were grave threats to mankind. By 1949 he'd even come to feel that the United States was capable of starting a war against the Soviet Union. After all, only a few years before, to end World War II, the U.S. government had dropped two atomic bombs that incinerated roughly 200,000 civilians in the Japanese cities of Hiroshima and Nagasaki. For Robeson it was logical that any public criticism he might make of Soviet policy would play into the hands of America's dangerously conservative right wing.

His judgment on that point never wavered (or, if it did, he never revealed it to anyone). To the end of his life Robeson would refuse to criticize the Soviets openly. He might tell close friends that "you can't make an omelet with breaking some eggs"—that, in other words, injustice to some individuals must always be expected, though regretted, in trying to create a new world that would improve the lives of the many. He continued to believe that the best chance for creating a more humane society lay with the egalitarian impulses originally unleashed by the Russian Revolution. Convinced that the Soviet Union was uniquely free of racial prejudice, Robeson saw no major Western power equally committed to the welfare of its minorities. Whatever private disappointment with the Soviet experiment he might have felt by the late 1940s, he resisted every pressure to turn it into public criticism.

In refusing through the years to criticize the Soviet

government, Robeson was refusing to give the Western powers any anticommunist ammunition that might strengthen what he saw as their racist control over the world's resources. But Robeson did sometimes exaggerate his criticism of the American government. In 1951, for example, in a petition to the United Nations, Robeson came close to saying that the institutional oppression of Black Americans was the same as a policy of official genocide, or deliberate destruction.

When Robeson attacked or criticized the policies of the American government, he always insisted that he was not attacking the American people. He constantly said that the real America was a progressive America and that the American people, good in their hearts, would ultimately set everything to rights. This underlying faith, in turn, has led Robeson's critics to call him naive. They have mocked his overarching belief in the "goodness" of the American people, saying it was just as mistaken and exaggerated as his criticisms of their government.

Yet Robeson was hardly naive. When the full extent of Stalin's crimes was published in the *New York Times* in 1956, Robeson read the article and then put down the newspaper without comment. His son later described his father's reaction this way: "He read it, he knew it was true," but "he never commented on it to my knowledge in public or in private to a single living soul from then to the day he died."

Robeson's reaction to the news probably fell into the middle ground of disappointed acceptance. He was disappointed that the Soviet experiment, so promising in the beginning, had been derailed by the acts of a dangerously unsound leader, but he continued to believe that in the long run socialism, still humanity's best hope, would triumph. The sheer number of Stalin's crimes and his policy of systematic murder did shake the faith of many in the communist camp, leading them to abandon their party memberships. Robeson, who had never been a member, remained loyal—not to Stalin's murderous regime but to the earlier, visionary ideals of international socialism that had guided the original 1917 revolution against the czars.

His was a complex temperament. Early on he learned not to trust anyone in the racist world into which he'd been born, yet he had a fundamental belief in the decency of most people. Unlike many Black Americans, he had not learned as a youngster to limit his expectations. His family had treated him like a god, and in the outside world he'd met far fewer humiliations than most Black people did. Optimism had become something of a core characteristic: he expected every set of hurdles to be cleared with hard work and determination.

Even as a young man, of course, Robeson had experienced enough discrimination and seen enough desperation in the Black world to know that society was cruel and individuals frail. Yet Robeson seems somehow never to have entirely digested the world's bad news. Over time he came to realize that social transformation would take longer than he'd originally thought, but he remained somewhat hopeful that one distant day humanity would rise to its better nature, that a cooperative social vision would supplant a ruthlessly competitive one, that human beings would somehow turn out better than they ever had, and that the principle of "connectedness"—the "human stem" being one, as he had once written—would hold sway in the world.

No other attitude would have allowed him to keep going. But

perhaps no other attitude could have been more likely in the long run to produce a traumatic breakdown, because it meant living with repeated, accumulated disappointments and denials.

"I'm Looking for Freedom"

When Robeson returned to the United States from Moscow in June 1949, the Council on African Affairs, which he chaired, staged a "Welcome Home" rally at the Rockland Palace in Harlem. Some five thousand fans, roughly half of them white, showed up to cheer his return. And he gave them their money's worth in one of the most powerful speeches of his career. "I defy any part of an insolent, dominating America, however powerful," he said. "I defy any errand boys, Uncle Toms of the Negro people, to challenge my Americanism because by word and deed I challenge this vicious system to the death. I'm looking for freedom—full freedom, not an inferior brand."

Most Black Americans, he insisted, unlike some of their leaders, were "not afraid of their radicals who point out the awful, indefensible truth of our degradation and exploitation. . . . How Sojourner Truth, Harriet Tubman, and Frederick Douglass must be turning in their graves at this spectacle of a craven, fawning, despicable leadership."

In thunderous tones Robeson went on to denounce the continued enslavement of colonial peoples and the betrayal of the Black American worker by some white labor leaders. He insisted that Black Americans "must have the courage to shout at the top of our voices about our injustices and we must lay the blame where it belongs and where it has belonged for over three hundred years of slavery and misery—right here on our own doorstep, not in any faraway place. . . . We do not want to die in vain any more on foreign battlefields for Wall Street and the greedy supporters of domestic fascism. If we must die, let it be in Mississippi or Georgia. Let it be wherever we are lynched and deprived of our rights as human beings."

Despite his challenging words, by the late 1940s Robeson felt increasingly penned in, no longer able to count on an admiring audience. Congress's House Un-American Activities Committee (HUAC) soon made that clear. Within weeks of his speech they subpoenaed him to give testimony.

When the day arrived, HUAC first called to the stand half a dozen Black witnesses hostile to Robeson. Alvin Stokes, a Black investigator for HUAC, claimed that the communists were planning to set up a Soviet republic in the Deep South and that "Robeson's voice was the voice of the Kremlin" (the seat of the Soviet government). Next up was Manning Johnson, a Black anticommunist and professional informer who'd done his masters' bidding in a number of earlier "loyalty" cases. He declared flatly and falsely that Robeson was a signed-up member of the Communist Party USA, had "delusions of grandeur," and wanted to become "the Black Stalin."

Johnson was followed by several more prominent Black citizens. Thomas W. Young, president of the Norfolk *Journal and Guide*, declared that Robeson had broken the bond he once had with Black people and had "done a great disservice to his race—far greater than that done to his country." Lester Granger, head of the Urban League, who'd already attacked Robeson in

Jackie Robinson testifying before the House
Un-American Activities Committee, 1949

print, somewhat surprised him by urging HUAC to investigate groups such as the Ku Klux Klan as well as suspected communists. That would "reassure the Negro leadership that while it is fighting against one enemy of this country, Communism, our Government is helping to fight off the other, Racism."

HUAC's final witness, its ace in the hole, proved to be none other than the Black baseball player Jackie Robinson. Six years earlier, Robeson had met with the owners of Major League Baseball clubs and passionately urged them to desegregate the sport. Two years after that, Robinson had become the first Black player on a Major League Baseball team in the modern era. Now he was a star—one whose appearance at HUAC would make headlines.

With movie and television cameras grinding away and the committee room packed with a standing-room-only crowd, Robinson read a prepared statement (apparently written for him by

Lester Granger of the Urban League). Robinson began by explaining that he'd decided to take part in the hearing out of "a sense of responsibility." He made it clear that Black Americans had real grievances and that police brutality and lynching were established facts. He praised Robeson as "a famous ex-athlete and a great singer and actor" who had the right to say, if he wished, that Black Americans would not fight in a war against the Soviets—though "it sounds very silly to me." Robinson added that Black people, in his opinion, "can win our fight without the Communists and we don't want their help." When Robinson finished, three HUAC members complimented him on his "splendid statement." He left immediately for New York, escaping, as one wit put it, "being Jim Crowed by Washington's infamous lily-white hotels."

The *New York Times* put Robinson's testimony on page one. For good measure, the paper ran an editorial the same day declaring, "Mr. Robeson has attached himself to the cause of a country [the Soviet Union] in which all men are equal because they are equally enslaved." The leading Black paper, the *Amsterdam News*, hailed Robinson for having "batted 1,000 percent in this game."

Not everyone agreed. At a Bill of Rights conference the following week, the 1,200 delegates gave Robeson a standing ovation. Another Black newspaper, *The Afro-American*, ran a cartoon depicting a frightened little boy labeled Jackie Robinson with a huge gun in his hand, uncertainly tracking the giant footprints of Paul Robeson; the caption read, "The leading player in the National Baseball League is only a tyro [beginner] as a big-game hunter."

Robeson's own reaction to Robinson's HUAC testimony was one of muted sadness. He called the HUAC proceedings "an insult to the Negro people" but announced that he would not "be drawn into any conflict dividing me from my brother victim of this terror." He insisted that he had only respect for Jackie Robinson and that Robinson was entitled to his opinion. Realizing that, in the context of the day, Robinson's statement had actually been mild, Robeson said that there was "no argument between Jackie and me."

As for Robinson, in his 1972 autobiography *I Never Had It Made* he wrote that he had no regrets about the remarks he'd made before HUAC. Yet in that same book he also wrote, "I have grown wiser and closer to painful truths about America's destructiveness. And I do have increased respect for Paul Robeson who, over a span of twenty years, sacrificed himself, his career, and the wealth and comfort he once enjoyed because, I believe, he was sincerely trying to help his people."

Panic in Peekskill

The very next month, in late August 1949, Robeson was scheduled to give a concert on the Lakeland Acres picnic grounds just outside of the town of Peekskill, located in upstate New York. Robeson had previously sung three times in the Peekskill area, always to an enthusiastic reception. This time would be wildly different.

No sooner was Robeson's concert announced than the Peekskill *Evening Star* ran a front-page story with a three-column headline: ROBESON CONCERT HERE AIDS "SUBVERSIVE" UNIT. The accompanying editorial blasted home the message: "The time for tolerant silence that signifies approval is running out." A rash of activity immediately followed, with the chamber of commerce leading the way in calling the forthcoming concert "un-American."

Peekskill was a blue-collar, working-class town, with pockets of well-off, left-wing sympathizers, mostly Jewish, who had summer places there—and were disliked and distrusted by the locals. Helen and Sam Rosen were among those summer visitors. On the day of the concert, the Rosens heard on the radio that various groups, including the Veterans of Foreign Wars and the American Legion, were mobilizing to protest. As arranged, Helen and her fourteen-year-old son John went to the train station to pick up Paul. As a precaution, Helen got a friend to put Robeson in his car and drive behind her.

While they were on the road, news came over the radio that protesters were massing at the local picnic grounds, the site of the concert. As they approached the grounds, a brawl was in progress. A truck had been deliberately parked in the middle of the road, effectively blocking it off and forcing traffic to a crawl—thereby allowing marauding groups of young men to check the occupants of each car, yanking some of the passengers out while a jeering crowd on the sidelines yelled "Dirty commie!" along with vile anti-Jewish slurs. People threw rocks at the passengers and mauled some of them.

The police were visible—but none made a move to interfere with the gathering mob. Some smiled. Helen saw a burning cross on the hill and promptly got her son down on the floor

Young men proudly displaying the destruction they caused after attacking concertgoers who had hoped to see a scheduled Paul Robeson concert in Peekskill, New York, on August 27, 1949. (The anti-Robeson demonstration was organized by the Joint Veterans Council of Peekskill.)

of the car. Then she ran to her friend's car behind hers, where Paul was. He was enraged and, according to Helen, "we had a hard time keeping him from getting out of the car." Helen finally yelled to her friend, "Get him out of here! Get him to New York!" That done, Helen and her son inched their way home while the sizable anti-Robeson mob attacked concertgoers, smashed the stage, torched the chairs around it—and put a dozen Robeson supporters in the hospital.

At a press conference the next morning at the Hotel Theresa in Harlem, Paul characterized the rioting as "a preview of

American storm troopers in action. . . . We'll protect ourselves, and good! . . . I'll be back with my friends in Peekskill!" The Rosens opened up their house in the Peekskill area for a protest meeting to plan strategy. Flooded with hate calls, Helen called the state police for protection. They promised to come—but never showed up.

Fifteen hundred people did appear at the Rosens' to declare their support. They formed the Westchester Committee for Law and Order and invited Robeson to return. Several left-wing unions pledged to mobilize their members to serve as a cordon of defense for a rescheduled concert. As soon as it was announced that Robeson planned to return to Peekskill, tension mounted. When Helen went into town to buy groceries to feed the union men guarding her house, nobody would talk to her. Flag salesmen appeared everywhere on the streets. Most vacationers closed up their houses and left for Manhattan. Two effigies of Robeson were hanged on the night before the rescheduled concert.

The next morning, union members arrived to set up defense lines at the concert site. The state police established a command post nearby, while a police helicopter circled overhead. By midday some twenty thousand concertgoers had begun to arrive. So had a large veterans' protest parade whose marchers yelled anti-Semitic and anti-Black remarks and taunted the concertgoers with shouted threats: "We'll kill you!" and "You'll get in but you won't get out!" A group of union guards ringed the stage.

As a prelude to Robeson's appearance, folksinger Pete Seeger sang and a famed piano duo played Bach and Chopin. There were no speeches, political or otherwise.

At four, Robeson, accompanied by his admittedly terrified pianist Larry Brown, opened the concert with "Let My People Go," then brought the crowd to its feet with "Ol' Man River." Helen noticed several men with guns take up positions on the ridge surrounding the stage; it was clear to her that Paul was an easy target in full view, and that he was quite literally taking his life in his hands. The trade-union guards flushed two men with high-powered rifles out of a nest on the hillside.

Somehow the uneasy truce held throughout the concert. When it was over, Robeson was taken out in a convoy of cars whose windows had been shaded with blankets. Robeson himself lay on the rear floor of a car, while two of the trade-union bodyguards covered him with their bodies.

Then the crowd started home. Or tried to. As the line of buses and cars crawled along the steep road winding out of the hollow where the concert had been held, it ran into a gauntlet of enraged locals, shouting "Go back to Jew town!" and "Get going, you Red bastard!" (Red was the color associated with international communism.) Some hurled rocks from the embankment, shattering the concertgoers' car windows. Flying glass injured many. Other locals stopped cars, dragged out the occupants, and beat them. The police did nothing to intervene. Some of the troopers joked with the anti-Robeson forces on the embankment. Others joined the attackers below.

Hundreds of the volunteer union guards were trapped in the hollow, surrounded by the stone-throwing mob and by a thousand state policemen, who refused to let the union men return to their buses. The threatening crowd encircled and then charged the trapped guards, beating them with their clubs, seriously injuring a number of them. A frantic call was put in to Governor Thomas E. Dewey. The governor's press secretary's curt response was that "a bunch of Communists had started violence"—and that the governor could do nothing.

The melee went on until 1:30 a.m. By the time it was over, dozens of cars and buses had been smashed and overturned, and 150 people had been injured seriously enough to require medical treatment. The Westchester County district attorney congratulated the police on having done "a magnificent job." That same DA, in his later report to Governor Dewey, concluded that "every precaution possible was taken to insure the safety of all present."

Governor Dewey issued a statement calling the concertgoers "followers of Red totalitarianism" and insisting that "Communist groups obviously did provoke this incident." The *Peekskill Star* compared the clash to the Boston Tea Party.

Several weeks later, the eleven communist leaders standing trial in New York were convicted and sentenced to five-year prison terms. As one of them said, "In the whole history of the United States, with more than 5,000 brutal and monstrous lynchings of Negroes, not one perpetrator had received a sentence of five months—to say nothing of five years."

From Bad to Worse

Bad news was soon arriving in batches. Early in 1950, Senator Joe McCarthy gave a speech in Wheeling, West Virginia, in which he deplored American weakness in the world and hinted darkly about the infiltration of the "enemy" into the highest levels of the State Department. McCarthy's vicious crusade against communism was just around the corner.

Robeson continued to travel and to speak out, but he found ever fewer outlets. His concert tour after Peekskill drew some fans, but fewer white people attended. In a number of cities, groups like the American Legion successfully organized boycotts that increasingly led to the outright cancellation of Robeson's scheduled concerts.

The world was narrowing for Paul Robeson. It would rapidly become narrower still.

Chapter 11

THE FIGHT FOR THE RIGHT TO TRAVEL

IF THE UNITED STATES WAS TURNING AGAINST Robeson in some ways, Europe remained more cordial. He made a quick trip to London in 1950 to speak and sing at various events, and he made plans to return for a longer tour at the end of the summer. The U.S. State Department had a different plan.

It issued a "stop notice" at all ports to prevent Robeson from traveling abroad, and internal security agents were sent to confiscate his passport. When Robeson refused to turn it over, the State Department immediately notified immigration and customs officials that the passport was void, or canceled. The officials were "to endeavor to prevent his departure from the U.S." if he tried to leave the country.

A crucial turning point had been reached. Robeson had now joined a number of other well-known radicals whose right to travel had been restricted, including the painter Rockwell Kent and the writer Howard Fast.

In the past, the State Department had given concrete reasons for denying someone a passport—the need, say, to prevent criminals from fleeing the country. But increasingly during the early 1950s, the department gave no reason at all, other than the vague explanation that "the best interests of the United States" were at stake. This was an obvious cover for monitoring and limiting left-wing political dissent. When Robeson's attorneys asked why his right to travel would not be in the country's "best interests," they were told that his frequent criticism of the treatment of Black people in the United States should not be aired in foreign countries. It was "a family affair."

No national outcry arose against the lifting of Robeson's passport. Not a single prominent Black leader protested. Robeson was being effectively isolated. When an attempt was made in September 1950 to book Madison Square Garden for an event marking the first anniversary of the Peekskill riot, the management refused to rent out the arena.

Robeson had greater support in Harlem. An outdoor rally sponsored by the Harlem Trade Union Council drew five to six thousand people. Harlemites could not be stampeded into an automatic anti-Soviet response; the "Red Menace" of communism did not strike many Harlemites as notably more dangerous than the white one.

But the country at large did not share Harlem's mood. The national press increasingly linked Robeson with another prominent Black dissenter, W.E.B. DuBois. When DuBois decided in November 1950 to run for the U.S. Senate, most of the Black leadership supported his opponent. Yet at a rally for DuBois at Harlem's Golden Gate Auditorium, Robeson was resoundingly applauded when he introduced DuBois as a man who stood against the determination of big business "to run the world, to make it over in the American Jim Crow, 'free enterprise' image—or ruin it."

DuBois got a respectable 13 percent of the 5 million votes cast in the election. Three months later, the Justice Department charged him as an "unregistered foreign agent" and set his trial for November 1951.

In the meantime, Robeson and DuBois combined their limited forces to put out a new publication, *Freedom*. Louis Burnham, a journalist who had been the director of the Progressive Party in the South, became its editor. And they had help—from Essie Robeson.

At this point, Paul and Essie had been living apart for some time, with Paul staying in the homes of various friends, including Sam and Helen Rosen. But the two had remained married, and Essie had grown to more closely share Paul's political views. She worked particularly hard to help make a success of *Freedom*—which the FBI immediately labeled "a Communist Party front organization."

Freedom began publication in December 1950. That same month, Robeson's lawyers instituted a civil suit for the return of his passport. The suit insisted that he was "a loyal, native-born American citizen" and argued that cancellation of his passport not only deprived him of his constitutional right of free speech but would also prevent him from practicing his profession and earning a living. Lawyers for the State Department countered that the department had always had the discretionary power to issue or refuse a passport. Both sides knew that they were in for a long and tortuous journey through the courts.

Act Together Now to Halt The Killing of Our People!

Robeson Calls for Unbreakable Unity in Face of Common Peril

By PAUL ROBESON

Vol. 2—No. 1   JANUARY, 1952   10c

HARRY T. MOORE lies in state for funeral service in Mims, Fla. church. Angry mourners converged on this little citrus town from over the state and as far away as New York. Photo by Russell Meek

Harry T. Moore died the death of a hero. He is a martyr in the age-long struggles of the Negro people for full dignity and equality. His name must never be forgotten and his courageous deeds must ever be enshrined in our memories. His death must be avenged!

The bomb which took the life of this fearless fighter for freedom, made a shambles of his home at Mims, Fla., and placed his wife at death's door in a hospital 40 miles away, has shaken the peace and tranquility of every Negro household in the United States.

There can be no mistaking the meaning of this event. The murder of Harry Moore was a lynching of a special kind. It was a political assassination.

Its aim was to short-circuit the growing clamor for votes and justice in the South by beheading those who are brave enough to demand their rights or strong enough to lead the organized mass movement.

In 1948 Maceo Snipes and Isaiah Nixon both gave their lives to Georgia mobs because they sought to exercise the right to vote.

In South Carolina, Albert Hinton, NAACP state president, was kidnapped, and John McCray, head of the Progressive Democratic Party was framed on a trumped-up libel charge—because of their leadership in the voting movement.

Only last month in Opelousas, La., John L. Mitchell was shot in cold blood by a deputized bandit because he had dared sue for his right to be registered as a voter.

SANFORD, Fla. — Forty-eight hours after Harry T. Moore was placed in his grave at Mims, Fla., his wife, Mrs. Harriet Moore, died in the Fernald Laughton Memorial Hospital here. As she joins her husband in martyrdom outraged Negro America cries out: "HOW LONG, O LORD, HOW LONG?"

(Continued on Page 6)

Harry T. Moore
Hero and Martyr

Dynamite Blast Resounds in UN

By WILLIAM L. PATTERSON

PARIS—The Christmas night bomb-killing of Harry T. Moore has had its reverberations all over the world, and especially in the councils of the United Nations General Assembly. The Assembly had recessed and most of its members had flown to their homes to celebrate the Christmas and New Year's holidays when news of this latest crime against the American Negro was flashed to every continent.

They would return to the UN sessions with one more ghastly proof—if any were needed—of the authenticity of the document which I had just submitted to the General Assembly in the Palais Chaillot. The document, "We Charge Genocide—the Crime of Government Against the Negro People" arms the whole of the world of decent men, women and youth with material that utterly destroys the lies scattered abroad by the rulers of America that

they have any title to moral leadership.

On Dec. 18 the Negro people of America placed this material in the hands of Trygve Lie, secretary-general of the UN; Luis Padilla Nervo, president of the General Assembly, and Mrs. Eleanor Roosevelt, chairlady of the Human Rights Commission.

The American Negro has no voice in the courts of Mississippi or any other Southern state. He has little or no voice in the North when a fundamental political or social issue is at stake. But here in the

(Continued on Page 7)

HATE-CRAZED "white supremacists" left this wrecked home in Mims, Fla., when they bombed Mr. and Mrs. Harry T. Moore to death as they lay in bed on Christmas night.

An issue of the newspaper Freedom, *jointly founded by Paul Robeson and W.E.B. DuBois*

Public Battles

If DuBois and Essie remained loyal to Paul, they were among the few well-known Black Americans who did. The famous boxer Sugar Ray Robinson, for one, told the influential *Herald Tribune* that anyone who doubted that the United States "provides opportunity for everyone, regardless of race, creed or color" was, like Robeson, simply mouthing "Communist propaganda."

Walter White of the NAACP launched a far more substantial attack in the pages of *Ebony*, the widely read Black magazine. White's attack was especially effective because, unlike many Black leaders, he had never indulged in a direct personal assault on Robeson. He now made up for lost time.

White charged Robeson with having a taste for luxury and a neurotic oversensitivity about racial "slights." He further claimed that Robeson lived in "magnificent" style in London's "exclusive Mayfair section." This was pure invention: the Robesons had never lived in Mayfair, and even if they had, the lack of a passport would have prevented their getting there. More hurtful still was White's charge that Robeson had done "little toward helping movements to correct the flaws in American democracy." This was malignantly false. Among much else, Robeson had been intensely involved with the Progressive Party and the trade-union movement.

A furious Essie took it upon herself to answer White and did so in hard-hitting style. Being stubborn in defense of one's rights, she told White, was neither "oversensitive" nor "neurotic"—unless, that is, you thought that the uncompromising stance the much-admired Indian activists Mahatma Gandhi and Jawaharlal Nehru had taken in their struggle for India's independence from Great Britain was also a symptom of "disturbance."

Perhaps it was past time, Essie suggested, for a hard look at the assumptions guiding the current crop of Black leaders in America. They don't dare claim that *Russia* is responsible for the entrenched bigotry against Black people in the United States. Instead they "go out of their way to insist that American democracy, with all its faults, is the best there is and therefore we must all fight and if need be die for it." *Ebony* refused to print Essie's response to White, but it did appear in the *California Eagle,* a sympathetic Black newspaper.

The NAACP's official publication, *The Crisis,* printed savage anti-Robeson articles in both its November and December 1951 issues. One, unsigned, simply dismissed Robeson as "a Kremlin Stooge." The other was a new attack by Roy Wilkins.

Soon after that, Robeson nearly came to blows at the Red Rooster Tavern in Harlem with Don Newcombe, the Black pitcher for the Brooklyn Dodgers. According to newspaper accounts, Newcombe reportedly shouted at Robeson that he was "joining the Army to fight people like you." At that Robeson lost his temper, and the two men had to be separated.

Essie responded to Newcombe in print: "Does he think Robeson is responsible for having kept him and [Roy] Campanella and [Jackie] Robinson out of big league baseball for so many years? Does he think Robeson is responsible for making him and the majority of the Negro people live under segregation and discrimination and persecution? All I can say is Don

Newcombe had better begin to talk and think for himself, if he ever wants to be more than a pitcher."

In this battle of words, W.E.B. Dubois had the last word: "The only thing wrong with Robeson is in having too great faith in human beings."

"Sympathy for My People"

On June 20, 1951, a federal grand jury in New York returned Smith Act charges against twenty-one more leaders of the Communist Party USA. Seventeen were arrested. At a mammoth Chicago Peace Congress at the end of the month, Robeson publicly declared himself "one hundred percent on the side of the condemned and arrested leaders."

So long as the Smith Act remained on the statute book, Robeson went on to say, "no other dissenter, whatever his politics, can feel safe in the exercise of the historic American right to criticize and complain"—to exercise, in other words, the First Amendment right to free speech. That night, as Robeson crossed the lobby of his hotel, the famous jazz musician Charlie Parker spotted him and grabbed his arm. "I just wanted to shake your hand," Parker said. "You're a great man."

Robeson was certainly a busy man, despite the State Department travel ban. When he could find a welcome mat, he continued to attend peace crusades, to speak on behalf of the Harlem Trade Union Council, and to help organize legal appeals relating to notorious racist cases.

Robeson's defiant words and actions continued to find far more response from abroad than from within the United States. From Bombay came word that he'd been vigorously applauded in absentia at the All-India Peace Convention, and from Paris that his was one of four huge pictures carried by the crowd in a Bastille Day parade. (The other three were Franklin D. Roosevelt, Abraham Lincoln, and Communist Party USA leader Eugene Dennis.)

At home, however, Robeson's reputation continued to slide. Some union halls and some Black churches still opened their doors for an occasional speech or concert, but now the announcement of his appearance in an American city routinely produced a wave of opposition. In 1952 the *Freedom* staff managed to cobble together invitations for Robeson to sing at some sixteen places, but only after much effort, and for minimal pay. (*Freedom* itself was able to struggle along for only a few more years.)

The organizers of a concert in Seattle, for example, had to send out special-delivery letters to Black clubs, churches, and political organizations that stressed the importance of "giving the lie" to city officials who'd announced that Robeson's appearance would create serious racial tensions. When the city then proceeded to cancel the contract for the civic auditorium, the pro-Robeson forces had to file a court injunction. They succeeded in getting permission to use the auditorium, but the Seattle authorities had the last laugh. Instead of an expected attendance of some 2,500, only 1,700 people bought tickets. The night's profits were a mere $250.

The rest of the tour—some fifteen cities—went still worse,

with considerable official harassment but little local support. In St. Louis the Black church sponsoring Robeson's concert withdrew its offer after city officials warned that "vandals" would be likely to wreck the church in reprisal. In Milwaukee, despite a house-to-house canvass, only a tiny audience showed up. The president of the University of Minnesota denounced Robeson as "an embittered anti-American" and canceled the concert—*after* tickets had been printed. In Pittsburgh, two FBI agents filmed the arriving audience.

Robeson's fees for these concerts averaged just three hundred dollars, compared with the two thousand dollars he'd once commanded. He pointed out, rather forlornly, that if he were indeed a communist, he would long since have been hauled before a congressional committee or a court. He *did* admire the Soviet Union, he said at one stopover, but primarily for its support of minority rights. "The real core of my fight," he accurately insisted, "is not political but is based on . . . sympathy for my people and for all colored people of the world. . . . The only thing we must concern ourselves with is Negro liberation."

McCarthyism and More

And then things got worse.

As public approval for Senator Joe McCarthy grew, he called for more indictments of second-level Communist Party leaders under the Smith Act. Nothing less, he thundered, would be sufficient to expose and contain the enormity of the Red Menace. When an American couple named Julius and Ethel Rosenberg were arrested and charged with espionage and conspiracy to transmit atomic secrets to the Soviets, hysteria rapidly mounted in the country. (The Rosenbergs would be convicted and, in 1953, executed.)

The anticommunist fever affected many aspects of American life. There were air-raid drills in the urban centers and calls in Congress for a preventive first strike against the Soviet Union— something that was seriously considered for a time. Adlai Stevenson, the "liberal" Democratic candidate for president in 1952, announced his support for the Smith Act convictions, for loyalty programs, and for the firing of "communist" teachers. Even so, the Republicans won a landslide victory in the election. The Progressive Party garnered about a fifth as many votes as it had in 1948. That was its last national campaign.

When Robeson again applied for a passport, the State Department again turned him down, announcing that it saw "nothing to indicate that Robeson's attitude has changed." Which was true. Robeson was not one to alter his convictions simply because they'd become inconvenient, even painful, for him. His main point throughout the long passport struggle was that the right to a passport did not and should not hinge on a citizen's politics. Under the Constitution, "attitudes" and opinions were not crimes. They were at the core of the country's protected heritage of free speech.

The government's case rested on a dubious interpretation of the president's war powers and the actual state of the current "national emergency." The racist underpinning of the government's charge against Robeson was revealed plainly in one of its 1952 legal briefs, when it described him as having been "for years

extremely active politically in behalf of independence of the colonial peoples of Africa. Though this may be a highly laudable
aim, the diplomatic embarrassment that could arise from the
presence abroad of such a political meddler, traveling under the
protection of an American passport, is easily imaginable."

Thwarted politically and contained artistically, Robeson relied more and more during the 1950s on his restorative relationship with Sam and Helen Rosen, with whom he stayed more
often than with any of his other friends. Sam knew about and
accepted the relationship between Helen and Paul, and he delighted in Paul's company almost as much as Helen did. Sam
and Paul would talk sports for hours, Paul taught football plays
to the Rosens' son, John, and, with their daughter, Judy, playing
the piano, he'd hold family recitals.

He'd often curl up for hours reading or studying—he was
learning Chinese calligraphy—taking occasional breaks to con-
sume what the family viewed as "mammoth" portions of ice
cream and peanut brittle. He and Helen would often take long
walks in the secluded stand of large fir trees surrounding their
country house. They'd talk dreamily of a world without bigotry
and war; or, sitting under a tree, Paul would put his head on
Helen's lap and drowsily sing her favorite song, "The Riddle
Talk."

In June 1953, Robeson made another effort to piece together
a concert "tour," but it failed to meet even the modest level of
the previous year. He focused his efforts on the Black community, his sole remaining base of support. That community's resources were limited, however, and even there not everyone felt
goodwill toward Robeson. Black people as a whole continued to

love and support him; many working-class Black people tended to feel that Robeson had been saying the things they would have liked to say, if they had a voice. The Black middle class, though, was more divided. Some admired Robeson but worried about alienating white allies.

Generally speaking, despite some critics, the Black world saw Robeson primarily as a champion of Black rights, not as the agent of a foreign power. If he was a "communist," it was with a small "c," someone who believed in a society where a much larger percentage of the people could share in its opportunities and rewards. Unlike J. Edgar Hoover and the FBI, most Black Americans did not see Robeson as a "Communist" with a capital "C"—that is, a registered member of the Communist Party.

To the average Black churchgoer, working for civil rights was an essential and proper part of the church's business. They'd heard over and over again that Robeson was a "godless" communist, but to them he didn't *sound* godless. He personified the spirituals in his music—nobody who "didn't have God in him," as one admirer put it, could sing "Deep River," a spiritual he'd sung in concerts and in the movie *Proud Valley*, the way Robeson did. Hadn't his father been a preacher? Wasn't his brother Ben also a pastor? Though Robeson never showed any particular devotion to the institutional church and was not religious in any formal sense, to many Black people he was an intensely spiritual man who drew strength from his deep cultural identification with his people, including their faith.

Still Fighting

As Robeson's isolation mounted and government surveillance of his daily movements intensified, the toll on his spirit and even on his health became more pronounced. Yet although Robeson had seen, and even come to expect, the world's every mean trick, he had an ingrained optimism about human nature—in its potential, that is, not in the crippled human product currently in abundance. Robeson believed that socialism would create an environment that would allow our better natures to emerge. The powers that be, however, have never had much tolerance for the Robesons of the world, for the champions of what might be. Those in power must always condemn those who bring a hopeful message of change, because they're seen as a threat to "things as they are."

Politically, Robeson identified primarily with the original idealism of the 1917 revolution in Russia, not with the Soviet Union in its current form, nor with the Communist Party USA, whose internal warfare and rigidity made him miserable. Like many other intellectuals of his day, he had taken from his early visits to the Soviet Union the overwhelming impression of a nation devoted to encouraging the cultural flowering of different peoples, including nonwhite peoples, within its borders—a policy opposite to that of the "melting pot" for which the United States officially stood. He had aligned himself with the Soviet Union in the 1930s because it seemed to play the most visible role in the liberation of American and colonial peoples of color. His loyalty was to the principles of Black liberation and socialism rather than to the ambitions of nations or parties. "I have shouted," he told a reporter for *The Afro-American* in March 1954, "and will continue to shout at the top of my voice for liberation, full emancipation."

And he did just that. In that same month he denounced U.S. military intervention in the Central American nation of Guatemala, loudly protested continuing persecutions under the Smith Act, and raised his voice angrily against the imprisonment of Jomo Kenyatta in an effort to cripple the Kenyan independence movement. "Is it 'subversive,'" he asked reporters, "not to approve our Government's actions of condoning and abetting the oppression of our brothers and sisters in Africa and other lands?"

In the same spirit, Robeson continued to fight for the return of his passport. Another round in that battle began in the spring of 1954. Coordinated campaigns in England and the United States drummed up petitions, letters, and cables to the State Department deploring Robeson's "domestic arrest." Messages of support arrived from around the world from, among many others, actor and director Charlie Chaplin, Nobel Prize–winning poet Pablo Neruda, and Irish physicist J.D. Bernal.

In England, a major "Let Robeson Sing" campaign grew by leaps and bounds. In the States, Robeson's fellow artists, including jazzman Thelonious Monk, folksinger Pete Seeger, and playwright Lorraine Hansberry, launched a "Salute to Paul Robeson" at the Renaissance Casino in Harlem; it produced an overflow crowd of more than a thousand. The State Department remained unmoved. It once again formally denied Robeson a passport, and FBI agents continued to monitor him closely.

Paul Robeson's cancelled U.S. passport

But cracks in the "anticommunist crusade" were finally beginning to appear. In December 1954 the Senate passed a censure vote against Senator Joe McCarthy, and a summit meeting of the Soviet and U.S. heads of states marked the beginning of a thaw. At the same time, the Supreme Court issued a series of decisions that modified the legality of loyalty-security laws and reaffirmed the rights of political dissenters to speak their minds. And in the landmark *Brown v. Board of Education* decision, the Supreme Court struck down racial segregation in the nation's public schools. These events did not automatically guarantee a new day, but they were signs that change was on the way—as would soon become apparent.

Robeson hailed the *Brown v. Board* decision as "a magnificent stride forward in the long battle of colored Americans for full equality." Yet he wasn't surprised when White Citizen Councils quickly arose in the South—councils that openly predicted violence if Black students tried to enroll in white schools. And the Supreme Court's shift to the left soon produced a counteraction: a shift to the right among southern Democrats and conservative Republicans, who united to defend racial segregation and to oppose "communism."

Just as signs emerged that the country might be awakening from its right-wing slumber, Robeson began to feel the negative effects, physically and psychologically, of years of confinement and ostracism. Something of a crisis arrived in 1955. A series of unusually appealing invitations from abroad, including an offer from a Soviet studio to star in a film of *Othello*, persuaded him to go to court once more in an effort to get his passport returned. Robeson's lawyers based the renewed claim on a June 1955 U.S. Court of Appeals ruling that "the right to travel is a national right," and took the case to a district court in Washington, DC, that had recently returned the passport of another left-wing figure. According to that ruling, the right to travel could not be withheld except by due process of law. It looked as if this time around Robeson might prevail.

The State Department was represented by a federal district attorney named Leo A. Rover, who argued passionately that Robeson's case was different. Rover claimed that "this man" (only once during the hearing did Rover refer to him as "Mr. Robeson") was "one of the most dangerous men in the world." Robeson was, said Rover, a direct threat to the security of the United States.

A threat because he was a "communist sympathizer"? No. With a bluntness that matched his racism, Rover made it clear that he viewed Robeson as "dangerous" because of his activity on behalf of independence for the colonial people of Africa, and his insistence on equality for Black Americans. The judge accepted Rover's argument and ruled against returning Robeson's passport. A higher court later decided not to overrule the decision.

Once again Paul Robeson had tried to reclaim his right to travel. Once again he had failed. And this time, the blow proved traumatic.

Chapter 12

BREAKDOWN AND REVIVAL

HAVING BEEN SINGLED OUT AS A DANGER TO THE country, Robeson despaired that he'd ever be allowed to travel abroad. For the foreseeable future, he remained a prisoner in his own country. To make matters worse, the assault on his reputation began to affect his health.

Six weeks after the judicial verdict went against him, Robeson noticed that he was passing blood in his urine. A specialist diagnosed a problem with his prostate gland and recommended surgery. At almost fifty-eight, Robeson hadn't been a hospital patient since the days of his college football injury. Helen Rosen later remembered that Paul was "frightened stiff." His nerves were raw from the passport fight and the built-up strain of years of FBI surveillance. Now he understandably feared what "might be done" to him in the hospital. In the last days before the operation he kept telling his son that "if something happens to me," please do this and that. He also revised his will.

Robeson did have a difficult operation. Several doctor friends, in fact, thought it had been "botched." The recovery period was painful, and he had to remain in the hospital for three weeks. When finally released, he decided to take up life again with Essie—which surprised many of his friends. One recalled the joking remark Robeson had once made: "I'll never be in *that* rocking chair."

Yet the decision to take an apartment together in Jumel Terrace, in Manhattan, made considerable sense. Essie had recently been diagnosed with cancer and had had breast surgery. With her typical grit, she'd told few people about the cancer, and she'd made a good recovery. Still, it was always possible that the cancer could return. Knowing that Essie had long wanted to put their household back together, Robeson felt he owed it to her to be more available.

Besides, Essie was immensely competent and efficient. Paul had reached a stage in life when, anxious and unwell, he no longer felt as drawn to romantic attachments and sexual adventures. He knew that Essie would manage and organize his life as no one else could and that, in return, she'd expect little more than the formal appearance of a marriage.

The year 1955 not only brought the passport defeat and the painful aftereffects of surgery, it also brought the closing down of both the Council on African Affairs and *Freedom*, the newspaper Robeson and W.E.B. DuBois had founded. At the same time Robeson began to show symptoms of what is now called bipolar disorder, which usually takes the form of alternating periods of mania—of extreme excitement and energy—and depression.

Robeson's first bout was primarily manic. He became a dynamo of intellectual energy. Much of it took the form of talking repetitively about what he claimed was a universal music theory based on the pentatonic scale (a musical scale that has five notes in each octave and is used in many kinds of music, including blues). Robeson insisted—to the point of obsession when he was agitated—on the universality of the pentatonic scale. He claimed it proved the commonality, or shared quality, of human experience.

One of the few people allowed to see him during these months was Helen Rosen. She recalled that he went "on and on about the pentatonic interconnection of practically everything." He sometimes stayed overnight at the Rosens' place; when he did, Helen slept with one ear cocked, concerned about what he might do. At four o'clock one stormy winter morning she discovered him trying to leave the house. When she asked him where he was going, he said he had to get a book to track down an idea he'd just gotten about his pentatonic theory. "He didn't know *what* he was doing," Helen recalled. He did improve—indeed, before too long he would appear entirely normal—but in Helen's opinion he would "never again be quite the same."

Two months later, Robeson's mania turned to severe depression, with the classic symptoms of confusion, fatigue, lack of motivation, paralysis of will, and inability to concentrate. Yet he refused to see a psychotherapist and simply stayed in his room at Jumel Terrace.

Just as Robeson seemed to have hit rock-bottom, he was again subpoenaed to appear before the House Un-American Activities Committee. His doctors advised him not to go; his family and friends feared he might break down on the stand. Yet Robeson insisted. Accompanied by Essie and Paul Jr., he left for Washington. Just before entering the hearing room, he

Robeson testifying before the House Un-American Activities Committee, June 12, 1956

appeared so depressed and vacant-eyed that it was doubtful he'd be able to testify.

To everyone's amazement, Robeson performed admirably. His steady, even sharp testimony was all the more remarkable because the committee did everything it could to goad and unnerve him during the stormy hour-long session.

"Are you now a member of the Communist Party?" asked the Republican representative from Ohio.

"As far as I know it is a legal party," Robeson responded, "a party of people who have sacrificed for my people."

Asked the same question a second time, Robeson tartly replied, "Would you like to come to the ballot box when I vote and take out the ballot and see?"

Pressed yet again, he replied, "I am not being tried for

whether I am a Communist. I am being tried for fighting for the rights of my people, who are still second-class citizens in this U.S. of America. . . . You want to shut up every Negro who has the courage to stand up and fight for the rights of his people."

What remained of civility soon gave way. "Why didn't you remain in Russia?" one committee member asked. "Because my father was a slave," Robeson angrily responded, "and my people died to build this country, and I am going to stay here and have a part of it just like you. And no fascist-minded people will drive me from it. Is that clear?"

Only once did the committee come close to landing a body blow. "I'm glad you called our attention to the slave problem," a member of the committee urbanely said. "While you were in Soviet Russia, did you ask them there to show you the slave labor camps?"

Robeson refused either to denounce or defend Stalin's crimes, choosing instead to place them in the context of the United States' crimes against Black people: "The Soviet Union's problems are its own problems," he thundered, pounding hard on the table. "I'm interested in the place I am in, the country where I can do something about it."

Back in New York, congratulations rolled in from friends and supporters. "You made such fools out of them," reported James Aronson, editor of the *National Guardian*. "The Negro Community is strictly in your corner." Perhaps most important, the confrontation did wonders for Robeson's spirits.

His passport status, though, remained unchanged. On the very day the Supreme Court granted a new trial to five left-wing defendants who'd been convicted under the Smith Act, it refused to hear arguments against a lower court's decision against reissuing Robeson's passport. That made him the only living American the immigration authorities were directed to prevent leaving the continental United States. He was not even allowed to go to Mexico or to other places that did not require American citizens to show their passports as proof of citizenship.

Slow Steps and a Backlash

Robeson's enforced inactivity coincided, ironically, with a quickening of hope among Black Americans following the Supreme Court's *Brown v. Board of Education* ruling that public schools must be desegregated. Yet that ruling did not bring the rapid dismantling of Jim Crow laws or an end to segregated facilities. Far from it.

The court had recommended a "go slow" approach—but even that proved too radical for the newly elected Republican president, Dwight D. Eisenhower. He not only refused to endorse the *Brown* ruling but publicly stated, "I don't believe you can change the hearts of men with laws or decisions."

If the federal government was cautious in its approach to *Brown*, the white reaction in the South was ferocious. On March 12, 1956, 101 southern members of Congress issued a "Declaration of Constitutional Principles" that called on their states to refuse to obey the desegregation order. Massive resistance quickly followed, from "pupil placement" laws designed to maintain segregation to outright violence. As press and pulpit rang with calls to protect the sanctity of the white race, a tide of vigilantism swept over the South.

On December 1, 1955, Rosa Parks had refused to give up her bus seat in Montgomery, Alabama, to a white man—and launched the Montgomery bus boycott. Black citizens refused to ride the city's public transportation, crippling the system. The protest energized widespread Black resistance to racism and catapulted Martin Luther King Jr. and his philosophy of direct but nonviolent action to the forefront.

Throughout these developments, Robeson could only applaud from the sidelines. Confined by the white ruling elite and shunned by most of the Black establishment, he'd been effectively neutralized. And he felt it deeply. On the few occasions when he was quoted in the press, he praised the Montgomery bus boycott as "magnificent" and strongly urged Black Americans to mobilize behind Martin Luther King Jr.'s leadership.

But it was as if Robeson's voice sounded in an empty echo chamber. A fair number of the younger generation of Black activists did not even know his name—or, if they did, it stirred some dim memory they couldn't quite grasp. Others vaguely recalled Robeson as a committed socialist who'd mistakenly thought the Soviet Union represented the vanguard of a more equitable society. Youthful activists often believe that they're inventing the world from scratch—and that those who came before them are irrelevant.

When Paul, Essie, and Paul Jr. went to Washington in May 1957 to take part in a large civil rights action called the Prayer Pilgrimage, Robeson was largely ignored. No call came from the leaders of the Montgomery bus boycott or from Martin Luther

King Jr. to meet—let alone to consult. Certainly they didn't want the name of a "discredited Soviet apologist" associated with their movement. They'd either never learned or refused to hear that the struggle for Black rights had always been at the center of Robeson's agenda. Yet the Montgomery organizers did invite Roy Wilkins and Adam Clayton Powell Jr.—two Black leaders who had ferociously attacked Robeson—to speak. An outraged Essie announced that "the more I think of the NAACP the more dangerous I think it is. They always calm the waters when something concrete and really good is cooking."

Bypassed at Home, Hailed Abroad

Earlier in the 1950s, Robeson had taken some comfort from the fact that his isolation had been imposed by the white power structure. During the second half of the 1950s, as a mainstream Black protest movement emerged within his own country, it hurt a great deal more to find himself treated as an irrelevant remnant of some well-forgotten era—when he was acknowledged at all.

To soothe his hurt, to make up for being bypassed—and possibly, too, as a symptom of his bipolar disorder—Robeson now and then struck a boastful note that would previously have been unthinkable in a man of such authentic modesty. In 1957, for example, when he was finally offered a few concert dates in California, he basked in the rare glow of approval. Wholly out of character, he praised his own excellent performance to interviewers. This was no more, possibly, than a perfectly human burst of vanity, or a mild recurrence of mania. Whatever the cause, even a hint of boasting would have appalled the younger Robeson, a man of generous, largehearted grace. In some essential way—just as Helen Rosen had sensed—his surety of purpose and emotional centeredness had been deeply shaken.

Some comfort and support, though, came from overseas. His many friends in England formed a National Paul Robeson Committee to push for the return of his passport. By the spring of 1957 the notables supporting the campaign included twenty-seven members of Parliament as well as a long list of writers, artists, musicians, and other distinguished figures. To cap off the campaign, a thousand people crowded into St. Pancras Town Hall to hear Robeson sing, his voice carried across the Atlantic by a new high-fidelity telephone cable. Press coverage was scanty, but Robeson felt profoundly grateful to his British friends for giving him back some sense of belonging and purpose.

Three months later, perhaps as part of a general softening of Cold War hostilities, the State Department finally granted Robeson an administrative hearing in Washington. It turned into a grueling six-hour marathon session. Asked again and again about his supposed Communist Party membership, Robeson again and again refused to answer personal and political questions that had nothing to do with his right to travel.

When the charade was over, the Passport Division concluded that Robeson's failure "to make a full disclosure" automatically halted the processing of his application. The stalemate remained unbroken. But then, unexpectedly, the State Department made its first concession to Robeson in seven years. It still refused to restore his passport, but it gave him the right to travel to Alaska, Hawaii, Puerto Rico, the Virgin Islands, the West Indies, Guam, and American Samoa—that is, places in the Western Hemisphere where a passport was not required of U.S. citizens.

Soon after, an invitation arrived from England. The famed Shakespeare Memorial Theatre at Stratford-upon-Avon wanted Robeson to star in a production of *Othello* the following year, which Robeson's lawyer thought might influence the State Department to return Robeson's passport. A few attractive invitations also began arriving from within the United States.

As pleased as Robeson was to receive his first "mainstream" opportunities in a decade, he remained vigilant about maintaining both the integrity of his political positions and his loyalty to friends who had been charged and imprisoned under the Smith Act. Nor would he dilute his insistence that Black Americans be given all the rights and privileges of first-class citizenship. An FBI report characterized him as "solid as a rock . . . with the 'supers' [super-left] all the way."

Here I Stand

Early in 1958, with the help of a longtime writer friend, Robeson published *Here I Stand*, a 111-page manifesto/autobiography. It amounted to a clear declaration to Black America that his primary allegiance was to the Black community, not to international communism.

"I am a Negro" read the first line of the book. On the second page he added, "I am an American." He also tried to explain why he had always refused "to give testimony or to sign affidavits" as to whether or not he was a communist: "I have made it a matter of principle . . . to refuse to comply with any demand of legislative committees or departmental officials that infringes upon the Constitutional rights of all Americans." He insisted that "my belief in the principles of scientific socialism, my deep conviction that for all mankind a socialist society represents an advance to a higher stage of life—that it is a form of society which is economically, socially, culturally, and ethically superior to a system based upon production for private profit—have nothing in common with silly notions about 'plots' and 'conspiracies.'"

In *Here I Stand*, Robeson cited Black trade unionists and the Black church, not the Communist Party, as the wellspring of his personal strength as well as the essential vanguard in the struggle for a more just world. He pointedly advised Black leaders to "rely upon and be responsive to no other control than the will of their people." White allies were welcome, but "the Negro people's movement must be led by *Negroes*."

Robeson put his faith in "aroused and militant" Black mass action. In the struggle for civil rights, he rejected "gradualism," the slow approach to the desegregation required by law, as simply another form of racism, pointing out that "in no other area of our society are lawbreakers granted an indefinite amount of time to comply with . . . laws." The insistence that progress must be slow, he argued, was "rooted in the idea that democratic rights, as far as Negroes are concerned, are not inalienable and self-evident as they are for white Americans."

In a clarion call to put aside "petty ways of thinking and

doing things" and to heal divisions within the Black community, he issued a transcendent appeal to end "all our differences" in the name of a "nonpartisan unity." In all these ways, *Here I Stand* foreshadowed the language and vision that militant young Black people would soon take up.

A Right Restored

Another sign of Robeson's return to public life came when Vanguard Records put him back in a commercial recording studio for the first time in seven years. According to Essie, "Paul was nervous as a cat," but the sessions went smoothly. The sound technicians were amazed that the quality of his voice was intact, and the Vanguard people were delighted with the overall product.

In April 1958, just in time for Robeson's sixtieth birthday, another breakthrough came in the form of a resolution by Actors' Equity, the professional union of actors. It urged the State Department to release Robeson's passport. His birthday was publicly celebrated in an astonishing twenty-seven countries—a concert in Mexico City, a recital of Robeson recordings in South Africa (where his music had once been banned), a special "Robeson Issue" of a Swedish literary magazine, a broadcast on Radio Tokyo, and more. Prime Minister Jawaharlal Nehru of India issued a proclamation hailing Robeson for having "represented and suffered for a cause which should be dear to all of us—the cause of human dignity."

Then in May, after a decade's absence from the New York

City concert stage, Robeson reappeared at Carnegie Hall for a sold-out concert. The crowd cheered his arrival, rose to its feet three times during the concert to cheer him again, and at the conclusion shouted and whistled its approval. Some critics felt that his voice had lost something of "its old glow," but all commented on his unchanged power over an audience—or, as one of them put it, "his "incomparable vigor of presentation and limitless charm."

Robeson regretted that the audience had been mostly white, so the following week he gave another concert to a sold-out crowd in Harlem. Two weeks after that, he performed at his brother Ben's Mother A.M.E. Zion Church. There he told the crowd that "a lot of the hard struggle is over. . . . I've been waiting for this afternoon just to come back to give my thanks here."

And then, at long last, came the best news of all. In June the Supreme Court ruled 5–4 that the secretary of state could not deny a passport to any citizen because of their political beliefs. It added icing to the cake by declaring that the Passport Division had no right to demand that an applicant sign an affidavit concerning membership in the Communist Party.

Suddenly it was all over. The State Department specifically acknowledged that the court's decision *did* cover Robeson's case. Two weeks later, smiling broadly, Robeson held up his passport so that a crowd of photographers could get a shot of it. He told them that the victory was not a personal one but rather "a victory for the 'other America.'" Essie told a friend, "We keep pinching ourselves, wondering if we'll wake up and find it all a dream."

Congratulations poured in from around the world. From England came a renewed invitation to perform at

Stratford-upon-Avon—indeed, to open the 1959 season, the hundredth anniversary of the Stratford Festival, in the lead role in *Othello*. Robeson accepted at once, and Essie started packing their bags for London.

In a symbolic touch, Paul insisted they cross the Atlantic on a British rather than an American plane. As it took off, Essie jotted down a few notes:

> *It has been an 8 yr. pull, struggle all the way, for this trip. Paul is . . . quiet, happy, relaxed, "on his way" at long last. He is humming, singing softly, trying out his voice. It's there, alright. . . .*

Chapter 13

BROKEN HEALTH

THE BRITISH PRESS AND PUBLIC GREETED ROBESON with immense enthusiasm. Newspapers described him as "euphoric," deeply content. Everywhere he went, people rushed up to shake his hand or to call out a welcoming greeting.

Professionally, too, Robeson was in instant demand, and his agent had to pick and choose among many offers. He settled initially for three half-hour appearances on British television, a British concert tour, and a contract to open the Stratford season in *Othello*. During the first few weeks in London Robeson socialized widely, including dinner with Peggy Ashcroft (who'd played Desdemona to his Othello in 1930) and with the Nigerian minister of internal affairs.

After a month's stay in London, Paul and Essie flew to Moscow, where they received an over-the-top welcome of rapturous applause and a sea of bouquets. The following day, eighteen thousand people filled the Lenin Sports Stadium for Robeson's first public concert in the Soviet Union in nine years. The event was televised, and Robeson wept openly at the warmth of his reception.

But not everything was cheers and flowers. The constant travel and relentless schedule of events, along with the continued presence of film crews, proved exhausting. When the Robeson party reached the resort town of Sochi, Robeson did little for three days but rest and sleep. Then a leisurely cruise along the Black Sea coast was followed by two weeks of luxurious seclusion in a government rest house. Yet a disturbing restlessness continued to mark Robeson's behavior. Old friends who visited felt that he was out of sorts: he "couldn't sit still or stop talking," one of them said, and his conversation included some uncharacteristic "boasting" reminiscent of his earlier bipolar distress. Doctors in the coastal city of Yalta recommended further rest.

Soviet premier Nikita Khrushchev and his family were vacationing at a lodge nearby and invited the Robesons for a casual visit. A few days later Paul and Essie were invited back for a more formal dinner that included several high-ranking Soviet officials and their families, along with the leaders of half a dozen countries then controlled by or allied with the Soviet Union: Bulgaria, Romania, East Germany, and more. Toasts were made all around. According to Essie, Paul was so moved that he was in tears.

Soon after, the Robesons returned to London and Paul embarked on a three-month concert tour of Britain. Larry Brown, as usual, accompanied him on piano, and another pianist, Bruno Raikin, shared the bill as a soloist. Though the reviews were favorable, Robeson wasn't feeling fully himself. He told Raikin that he felt "a nervous wreck."

Raikin had already concluded that Robeson "wasn't as happy a person, as fulfilled a person, as he had been in 1949." That might simply have represented the ordinary decline of energy between ages fifty and sixty. Yet it seems to have been a sign of something more—especially Robeson's new habit of talking frequently to concert audiences, between songs, about the pentatonic scale and "the universality" of all folk music. It was a low-grade reappearance of the restless talkativeness of his earlier bout of full-blown mania.

In addition, he began to have unexplained bouts of dizziness. He confessed to Essie that he'd been feeling under "continuing strain," and that he was concerned that he might not be able "do all the things he finds himself agreeing to do." Worry, Essie reported, "has got him down."

"Off the Merry-Go-Round"

Essie had also become unwell again, and tests showed a "precancerous condition of the mouth of the uterus." She decided that it was time for both of them "to step off the merry-go-round, and collect ourselves and re-organize our lives, especially our health."

In Moscow, where they'd returned at Khrushchev's invitation to attend a formal New Year's Eve party, she and Paul decided to check into private rooms in the Kremlin Hospital for thorough checkups. Essie was started on a course of treatments involving radium that required her to lie still for twenty-four hours after each treatment—which, characteristically, she did faithfully and without complaint.

For Paul, the doctors prescribed total rest for a minimum of ten days. He obeyed them but then, according to Essie, "turned 'mulish.'" Part of his disquiet revolved around misgivings he'd had from the beginning about again taking on the role of *Othello*. In the hospital he'd continued to have bouts of dizziness, and Essie reminded him that the *Othello* role demanded sudden, vigorous movement. She thought it was "madness" to undertake the part. Paul finally agreed. He cabled Glen Byam Shaw, who ran the Stratford Festival, that he had no choice but to cancel.

Shaw begged him to reconsider and not to "ruin" the Stratford season. He also promised to adjust rehearsal and performance schedules to minimize the strain on Paul. By that point he was beginning to feel stronger physically, and in early February 1960 was able to leave the hospital for a month's stay in a plush rest home for Russian officials. Essie stayed on at the hospital for more treatments.

The more energetic Paul felt, the more he saw the Stratford *Othello* as an ideal way to get back into harness on terms that would limit the risk to his health and reputation. With due advance warning to his colleagues and the press, he could concentrate on the vocal aspects of the role, with which he felt comfortable, and minimize the physical movements that concerned him.

With Essie in agreement, Paul wired his acceptance to an ecstatic Byam Shaw. To spare Paul, Essie put off telling him until the last minute that her doctors insisted she complete the course of treatments before joining him midway into the rehearsal period.

Othello Once More

Rehearsals began less than a month before *Othello* was scheduled to open on April 7, 1959. Accompanied by a servant he'd known from his earlier days in England, Robeson moved into a suite of rooms in a grand farmhouse on the outskirts of Stratford. Its owner, a Mrs. Whitfield—described as "a very old-fashioned sort of English lady"—was charmed by his courtesy and became devoted to him. A Whitfield family member describes Robeson as filled with "personal happiness" throughout the rehearsal period.

Tony Richardson, the twenty-seven-year-old director of *Othello*, was known as an innovator. However, he settled for the traditional interpretation of Othello as the Noble Moor brought down by the foul deeds of an alien world. It was a decision that played to Robeson's strengths: a dignified, honorable Othello was the only one Robeson would be interested in playing, and probably the only one he could play. Robeson was the kind of actor who dramatized aspects of his own temperament; he lacked the technique to inhabit a character notably different from his own.

Unfortunately, Richardson went in very nearly the opposite direction regarding other aspects of the production. He filled the stage with flashy special effects, including rock-and-roll drumming and Great Danes dashing across the footlights, that clashed with Robeson's dignified seriousness. Under Richardson's direction, the actors playing the other two main characters, Iago and Desdemona, performed in a contemporary style that made Robeson's sonorous tones and serious demeanor appear old-fashioned and out of step.

The critics, though, mostly took Robeson's side. They denounced the gimmicky production and praised his traditional approach to the role. Several of them congratulated him on rising above the tricky superficiality of the production.

Robeson himself felt deeply relieved. Given the obstacles of a production at odds with his acting style, a serious recent illness, and the many years that had passed since he last appeared in a play, he felt extremely fortunate to have come through so well. Essie had been there for the opening and thought it a "terrific personal triumph."

Othello was also a commercial hit. Its seven-month run immediately sold out, and long lines formed nightly in the hope of last-minute tickets. Many friends, old and new, came to see Robeson's performance, including Helen and Sam Rosen, W.E.B. Dubois and his wife Shirley Graham, Peggy Ashcroft, Joshua Nkomo of Rhodesia, Oginga Odinga of Kenya—and Robeson's Rutgers sweetheart Gerry Neale, now Gerry Bledsoe.

True to his word, the producer gradually reduced the number of Robeson's performances after the first few weeks, with Robeson's understudy filling in for him. The lighter schedule gave Robeson plenty of time to rest, and also time for other engagements. Requests for his appearance came thick and fast. The BBC featured him in a series of ten Sunday night radio broadcasts and also offered a biography titled "The Paul Robeson Story." On television, he appeared with classical violinist Yehudi Menuhin and British jazzman Johnny Dankworth.

Robeson also marched with Peggy Ashcroft in a procession

*Paul Robeson speaking to a crowd in Trafalgar Square,
London, at a 1959 rally in support of nuclear disarmament*

through the town of Stratford to commemorate Shakespeare's
birthday; joined another old friend, the deported American
communist Claudia Jones, at the West Indian Caribbean Festival; took part in the African Freedom Day concert sponsored
by the Movement for Colonial Freedom; and sang at a huge
disarmament rally in Trafalgar Square. He even made a forty-
eight-hour trip to Prague to attend the Congress of Socialist
Culture. Speaking at the Youth Festival in Vienna, Austria, he
told the crowd that he believed "the future of the whole world
rests on socialism." He spoke, too, of his disappointment at the
rising tide of white resistance to desegregation in the American
South, of the fact that "eighteen millions of us do not have full

181

Paul Robeson with African and Asian students at
the World Youth Festival in Vienna, 1959

freedom." FBI legal staff members abroad dutifully kept J. Edgar
Hoover informed of Robeson's activities and views.

Paul played his last performance of *Othello* on November 26
and was called back for ten curtain calls. He hadn't missed a single scheduled performance in seven months, but the grind had
taken a greater toll than he publicly acknowledged. "It's been
wonderful," he wrote to Helen Rosen, "but a constant hazard.
The going has been tough. . . ." He confessed that he'd become

so lonesome for her sometimes that he'd "debated flying over (really) in between engagements." When his old co-star from the 1930s, Flora Robson, came to see a performance, he confided to her that he'd been having great difficulty remembering his lines and had to have a prompter at hand at all times to remind him if need be.

When the curtain came down on the final performance, Paul and Essie decided on a complete rest and medical checkups in Moscow before he began a three-month concert tour with Larry Brown. Essie had been struggling with her health, although she'd kept that from Paul. She wrote the truth to Helen and Sam Rosen, telling them that although she was finally beginning to get her energy back, she still came down with periods of "terrific and blinding pain."

The doctors in Moscow put Essie through a rigorous series of tests and found an "ulcerated" area high on the wall of the rectum. It would be difficult, though not impossible, to treat. She settled in for an extended period of therapy that would continue after Paul returned to London. His own health was found to be "very fine," give or take some extra pounds (he'd gone up to 280) and a tendency to tire easily. The U.S. embassy in Moscow was less pleased about Robeson than his doctors were. It reported to the State Department and the FBI that he'd several times publicly applauded recent Soviet government actions.

After returning to London, Robeson then set out on the thirty-two-city concert tour of England. The performances were praised, but ticket sales were somewhat disappointing. Talking with reporters at various stops on the tour, Robeson struck something of a farewell note. The success at Stratford, he told them, had given him a sense of artistic fulfillment. He did hope to continue performing but had no "startling plans."

One friend who hadn't seen Robeson in a while was shocked at "how much he'd aged and how tense he was." Another sensed "a keen desire on his part to get back to America"—and, in particular, to participate in the growing civil rights movement.

Yet Robeson realized that he had been tarred with the brush of "communism" and that the new generation of activists, including Martin Luther King Jr., would want to steer clear of that old battle. They would not be eager to seek him out. It made him sad, he wrote to Helen Rosen: "It all gets a little desolate now and then—no matter how wonderful things are in general." Once, while making a speech in which he referred to "my country," Robeson blurted out that "any time my folks say they need me, if it's tomorrow morning, I'll get back there, don't worry, bet your life I will."

Mixed Signals

Though Robeson yearned for home, the signals he got from the States were mixed. Almost daily he read accounts of the spread of sit-ins and the birth of the Student Nonviolent Coordinating Committee (SNCC), an activist group that helped organize sit-ins and other protests. A more militant phase in the Black struggle was under way, and sympathy for it was growing among liberal white northerners. In Africa, too, the demand for freedom was rapidly accelerating. Starting with Ghana's successful revolution in 1957, some dozen African nations had gained their independence within a few years.

In a letter to A. Philip Randolph, Robeson wrote that he'd "avidly followed" plans for the creation of a Negro Trade Union Congress, and complimented Randolph on having "so wisely led" the Pullman Porters. He praised, too, "the growing unity of Negro and white American youth in breaking down the tottering walls of segregation and discrimination." He even expressed the poignant hope of being "able to greet you in person in the near future." There is no known reply from Randolph.

Robeson did not view the 1960 election of President John F. Kennedy as good news. When asked by a reporter whether he thought Kennedy represented "the other America," Robeson's response was, "Maybe you'd better define what you mean by the other America."

He then gave his own definition: "The other America for me is Jefferson, Lincoln, Harriet Tubman, Frederick Douglass, Franklin D. Roosevelt. Kennedy is just about as dangerous as anybody else. He does not represent the Democratic Party's great traditions, but is, like Nixon, a firm supporter of NATO [the North Atlantic Treaty Organization, formed to counter the Soviet Union] and he wants more [military] bases, not fewer." As always, peace, for Robeson, was an important measure of progress.

More Travel, More Trouble

"In a socialist country," Robeson once said, "I give my services for free. In a capitalist country I charge as much as I can." He put that principle to work when a lucrative offer came through for a ten-week tour of New Zealand and Australia. He had no desire to go, but when he was guaranteed more than a hundred thousand dollars for twenty concerts, with additional sums for television appearances, he reluctantly accepted.

The tour did bring in the promised income, but it also turned into something of an ordeal. In Robeson's opening press conferences in the Australian cities of Sydney and Brisbane, several hostile reporters bombarded him with sharp-edged questions, and Robeson replied in kind. Asked if the condition of Black people had not greatly improved of late, Robeson shot back, "It has *somewhat* improved," primarily because Black people had become more militant in demanding their rights, and because the USSR supported the Black struggle.

Was he bitter about the way the U.S. government had treated him? That question set off an "emotional outburst." "If someone did something bad to me, I wouldn't be bitter," Robeson thundered—"I'd just knock him down and put my foot into his face."

This was not the easygoing, controlled Robeson of yesteryear. "He is angrier than ever," Essie wrote a friend, "and it makes me shudder, because he is so often angry at the wrong people, and so often unnecessarily angry." What Essie implicitly meant was that Paul's anger wasn't a response to immediate events. It represented the stored-up griefs and harassments of the past, and was a sign of a nature unraveling.

Something more was at play as well. When Essie mentioned the possibility of stopping off in the Philippines on their way back to London, Paul flew into a rage, insisting that U.S. agents would kill him if he ever set foot in the Philippines. Something had come unstuck in Paul. The effect of decades of abuse hurled at his head could no longer be concealed. The Australian press saw the danger signs and wrote headlines that might have jarred even someone who was not already on the edge. One proclaimed that Robeson WOULD BACK RUSSIA IN A WAR. Another headline read: ROBESON BITTERLY CRITICAL OF U.S.

In New Zealand, the press was far more polite, and Robeson's good nature resurfaced. When given a traditional welcome by the Maori, the native people of New Zealand, he described them warmly as "a wonderful people. . . . They have accepted us as of them and are very proud of our success. . . . Am over the dumps (the bad spots)—and riding high."

But he wasn't. Even in the more cordial New Zealand atmosphere, the embers continued to smolder. The press again commented on Robeson's "edginess . . . an impatience at any side-tracking." At one point he announced that he had no further musical ambitions, and that he wanted to be sufficiently fluent in any other language than English so "that I am not forced, as I am now, to do all my thinking and talking in the tongue of my oppressor."

Robeson sometimes talked politics even when the reporters hadn't asked him to. He criticized the United States for supporting Franco, the fascist dictator of Spain, and Chiang Kai-shek, leader of the anticommunist forces in China. He seethed over the mistreatment of the Maoris and the suppression of their culture and even expressed disappointment that Black Americans back home seemed wholly wedded to a prayerful, nonviolent struggle.

Essie reported to Helen and Sam Rosen that "your boy is full of bile and tension, and remains ANGRY at the drop of a hat. I'm very tired of coping with it. . . . You can have him. He's tired out, but keeps on doing everything on the horizon. . . . He resents everything I do, no matter what. So, I'm up to here. Period."

In some moods Paul himself recognized that he wasn't fully in control of his own emotions. "I wish I could be sweet all the time," he poignantly told a friend. "Sometimes what you read in the paper sounds a little rough. You're right, it was rough. That's right. I said it . . . there is little excuse not to function without seeming very difficult."

Unbearable Loneliness

Robeson returned to London thoroughly exhausted and swore that he'd never do another tour. He'd proved all he needed to prove, he said. His bank balance was fine. His artistic reviews (if not his political ones) had been excellent. He felt "just tired out."

To be "perfectly honest," he confessed, additional praise meant nothing when compared with "the *absolute vacuum* [emptiness] in my personal life." He felt "terribly, terribly lonely." It was "almost unbearable."

Robeson was still able to follow political events, though they hardly improved his mood. He scoffed at President Kennedy's interference in the politics of Laos, a Southeast Asian nation that had been drawn into the conflict between communist and anticommunist forces in neighboring Vietnam, and he reacted with fury to the assassination of Patrice Lumumba, the first prime minister of the newly independent Republic of Congo, who'd sought Soviet help in quelling a civil uprising after the United States and the United Nations had turned him down.

Robeson also protested vigorously against the imprisonment of his old friend Jomo Kenyatta in Kenya—accused of helping to organize a bloody uprising against white colonial settlers. "Let him be free, NOW, AT ONCE," Robeson wrote, "to take his rightful and dearly-won place; to give his courage, knowledge and perception to his too long suffering folk." (Kenyatta would be freed and would lead Kenya through most of the 1960s and 1970s.)

Gradually, Paul and Essie made plans for the rest of 1961. Paul would go alone to Moscow for a visit and then to Scotland for the Scottish Miners' Gala in Edinburgh. Later they would both go to the Prague Music Festival, to East Berlin, and then to Ghana and perhaps elsewhere in Africa. These would be visits, not concerts, and not overly tiring. Essie wanted to settle permanently in London, but Paul, feeling "completely desolate," wanted to return to the United States. He even felt briefly better about President Kennedy, saying that "he seems to be at least realistic and some of the people around him *are* decent. Let's hope."

But that note of optimism soon gave way. Robeson grew dismayed over what he took to be a split between middle-class and working-class Black Americans, and the refusal by the middle-class ones to "be caught anywhere in the deep left." It all made him feel "terribly lonely," he wrote to Helen Rosen, "but just doing the best I can. Have altogether failed to find friends over here. Guess I'm to blame . . . [Sam Rosen] is so sweet about me—and so disturbed when I'm raging and ranting. Both he and you are right—it means some '*inner*' disturbance."

He closed that letter on a note that struck Helen as suspiciously manic, however tender: "Thank you Lord. Thank you! . . . Thank you Lord! For such a lovely family [the Rosens] and you thank them too for taking me in. . . . I *do* love you—*adore* you—*cherish* you."

Helen's instincts and experience told her that Paul was in serious emotional trouble. She confided her fear to Sam, and they contacted two of the left-wing doctors who had treated Paul in the past. All agreed that he was not only on the edge of a breakdown, but that he needed to come home. It was decided that Helen should go immediately to London to check on Paul's state of mind.

She found him deeply troubled but not feeling well enough to return home. Essie, for her part, was firmly against returning to the States. One day when Helen arrived for a lunch that had been arranged, Essie told her that Paul had left by plane for Moscow. Even years later Helen was still unable to piece together the puzzle of his departure. Had Paul, on impulse, himself decided on the Moscow trip? Had Essie played a role in encouraging him? The details remain a mystery.

All that is indisputably clear is that on March 27 Essie got a call from Moscow: Paul had slashed his wrists.

Mental Illness

They couldn't tell Essie much when she arrived in Moscow. There had been a noisy party in Paul's hotel room, from which he'd retreated into the bathroom, where he cut his wrists with a razor blade. The trigger may have been, according to a psychiatrist Paul saw two years later, that "people whose parents or whose relatives were in jail had approached him—'Can't you help me?'—this sort of thing had put him into conflict."

When Paul Jr. arrived in Moscow a few days later, he wore himself out trying to find a logical explanation for what had occurred. Because Paul Jr. saw his father as a towering figure immune to ordinary emotional problems, he searched for evidence of some kind of external "plot" to do away with his father. He thought the U.S. Central Intelligence Agency (CIA) was the most likely villain. However, people he talked to who'd had recent contact with Robeson could provide no evidence to confirm his theory.

The team of Soviet doctors who cared for Robeson after he was brought to the hospital offered a confident diagnosis. "depressive paranoid psychosis." They told Paul Jr. that his father "had been so paranoid when first admitted" that he thought he was going to be killed; he'd even accused Essie of being a spy. Certainly the well-documented depressive bouts of the preceding year seem to support the Soviet diagnosis.

Paul Jr., however, continued to search for evidence that his father had been deliberately "neutralized." His frantic search brought only a dangerous increase in his own level of anxiety. Twelve days after arriving in Moscow, he himself broke down. Terror-stricken and hallucinating, he heaved a huge chair through the plate-glass windows of his hotel and nearly threw himself after it. He claimed that he, too, had been the victim of chemical poisoning by the CIA.

Essie's public explanation for Paul Sr.'s collapse centered on years of overwork in combination with "a slight heart attack." A counter-rumor began to spread that Robeson had attempted suicide because of disillusionment with the Soviet Union. But those who knew him best reject that explanation, and little has come to light to support it in the years since. Robeson's disillusionment, such as it was, was not with the Soviet Union in and of itself but rather with the way the world worked, with its refusal to move toward socialism as he had thought it would.

Robeson's sense of blighted hopes, personal and historical, was general, not limited to any specific disappointment, but his forlorn sense of loss was part of a bipolar depressive disorder. It's impossible to know for certain, but perhaps without the accumulated pressure of government harassment and worldly disappointments, any underlying tendency to depression might never have been activated; almost anyone who'd lived under pressures like those Robeson had experienced might have suffered a breakdown. It may be that all Robeson knew about the deepening malaise of the past few years was that his moorings had slipped. Abroad he now felt himself a stranger in unfamiliar territory; at home he felt bypassed by the civil rights movement he had done so much to forge.

Within a few weeks, both father and son were doing notably

better, and the doctors were much encouraged. A month after Paul Sr.'s attempted suicide, the two were transferred to the Barvikha Sanatorium for further rest. Ten days later, Paul Jr. was able to fly home to the States. The week after that, Paul Sr. was allowed to return to London, though with strict instructions for a prolonged rest.

Within two weeks of Paul's return to the flat he shared with Essie in London's Connaught Street, his mood again took an abrupt turn downward. Essie made a split-second decision to take Paul back to the Barvikha Sanatorium in Moscow. When their plane landed, friends reported that they'd seen Paul being carried from the plane by two white-coated attendants. Essie promptly sent out cheery notes to assorted friends and family, saying that it was simply a matter of having returned too soon to London—they'd gone back to Moscow to ensure a solid convalescence.

Helen Rosen got one of those chipper notes about "how very pleased" the doctors were with Paul's progress, and saw right through it. She and Sam were already nearby, in Romania, for a medical conference, so they decided to have a look for themselves. In mid-August 1961 they arrived at Barvikha for a planned stay of four days.

At the first sight of Paul, Helen was profoundly upset. He seemed utterly lethargic, as if drugged. Essie's singsong attempts to rouse him—"Let's show Helen and Sam how nicely we do our exercises"—only added to her concern. Essie tried to persuade the Rosens that the breakdown had occurred only after they'd returned to Barvikha, that it duplicated Paul's collapse in 1956, and that it was simply the result of "nervous exhaustion and tired heart." Helen and Sam had to leave after a few days to fulfill medical obligations, though they did so reluctantly.

This time around, Paul's "recovery" was slow and discouraging. Only after a full three months at Barvikha did the doctors decide to risk allowing him to go back to the London apartment. They also urged Essie to arrange for his return to the States as soon as possible.

That turned out to be a wildly optimistic scenario. Paul had barely been back in London for forty-eight hours when he had his most serious relapse yet. The usually unflappable Essie put in an emergency call to Helen in New York, pleading with her to come immediately to London. Helen dropped everything, took the next plane, and arrived in London the following morning. She found Paul curled into a fetal position on the bed, tangled up in the sheets, "positively cowering" in fear. Essie had already arranged for Paul to enter the Priory, a private facility said to be the best psychiatric hospital in England.

At the Priory he was put under the care of Dr. Brian Ackner, a highly regarded specialist. Ackner wrote in his notes that Paul was "in an agitated state with many ideas of persecution" and expressing "ideas of . . . unworthiness which . . . were quite delusional in the degree to which they were held." After tests and consultations with other experts, the doctors diagnosed Paul's underlying condition as "depression in a manic depressive personality."

Ackner decided to begin a course of electroconvulsive therapy (ECT), a procedure that consists of passing small electrical currents through the brain of a sedated patient. It was the preferred treatment for "major depressive" illness in the 1960s, and even today, when many more antidepressive medications are available, it's commonly used for severe depression and distress, especially for patients unresponsive to medication. Paul was highly sedated before each treatment and remembered nothing afterward.

Essie decided not to tell Paul Jr. about the seriousness of his father's condition. She feared it might have a negative effect on his own health, and she wanted to avoid having an explosive Paul Jr. underfoot. When he later learned the truth, he became furious with his mother. As she'd expected, Paul Jr. was convinced that the Priory was involved in a deliberate attempt to "neutralize" his father—a plot that he insisted was directed by the CIA and MI-5, the American and British intelligence agencies. No evidence has ever surfaced to support such a conclusion, but Paul Jr. continued to cling to it through the years.

Helen Rosen later tried in vain to explain to Paul Jr. that use of shock treatments had seemed inescapable at the time. Robeson had failed to respond to the few medications then available to treat his condition, and his extreme suffering called for immediate relief. Robeson did respond well immediately after each ECT treatment, which led his doctors to continue them, though in the long term the lasting benefits were uncertain.

At the height of the crisis, Helen spent a month in London, living with Essie in the Robesons' flat. After she uneasily returned to New York, she and Essie frequently exchanged detailed letters about Paul's condition. Unlike the bland reassurances she sent to others, Essie shared with Helen the full truth.

In early February 1962 Essie confided in Helen that Paul had again become "very depressed" and had started talking about finding a "short, fast way out." She repeated a conversation with Paul in which he had insisted "it wasn't worth it. Nobody could help, they tried their best, but he was sick to death of the struggle. If I was loyal, I would help [him die]. I agreed, but said first I must be sure there is no help. We must be sure we have tried everything. He agreed to that."

Robeson's alarmed doctors decided on a second series of eight ECT treatments to add to the sixteen he'd already had. Within ten days the improvement was so pronounced that he was asking for the newspapers, sleeping better, and writing to his business manager to say "he'd turned the corner—am sure will be all right from here on in."

A few weeks after that, when Essie told Paul that she was going to see singer Ella Fitzgerald's show with saxophonist Coleman Hawkins, he surprised her by saying he'd like to come along. And he did. When Fitzgerald spotted him in the audience, she quietly announced that she wanted to dedicate her next number to "her fellow artist and a very great man, Paul Robeson." When the performance was over, Paul amazed everyone by saying that he'd like to go backstage to greet and thank Ella. According to Essie, Ella was "thrilled," hugged and kissed him, said it was "a big day" in her life, and expressed joy that he seemed to be so much better.

The outing having gone so well, Paul repeated it four days later, this time with a trip to the Aldwych to see Peggy Ashcroft and John Gielgud in Russian writer Anton Chekhov's play *The Cherry Orchard*. That reunion also went well, yet afterward Paul told Essie that although he felt fine, he wanted to go back to the

Priory, not to their flat. He didn't want people to think he was "available" and start "having plans for him again."

A New Routine

What followed for many, many months was a pattern of shuttling back and forth between the flat and the Priory. The amount of time Robeson spent at the flat depended on his apparent improvement—and also varied with his tolerance for being cooped up with Essie.

He'd long considered enforced daily life with her to be something of a nightmare, with her controlling temperament and her constant hovering. For thirty years he'd managed to avoid being locked up with her for any length of time, and he'd always relied on others to arrange the bothersome details of daily life. Now, in his sixties and distrustful of his own soundness, he had to rely on Essie's judgment about many things—like whether he should take a nap. Daily irritability on both their sides was unavoidable, but no serious eruptions took place. For one thing, Paul was incapable of anything as strenuous as a major argument. For another, Essie put his comfort above all else. She did everything in her considerable power to prevent demands on his limited ability to cope. He was extremely lucky to have her, and her loyalty to him was unswerving

The world left Paul alone, but it hadn't entirely forgotten him. His sixty-fourth birthday, on April 9, 1962, brought greetings from around the world. Helen called from New York, thrilled that his voice sounded "so deep and quiet." And Kwame

Nkrumah of Ghana wrote to suggest that Robeson settle in Ghana, as W.E.B. Dubois and Shirley Graham had recently done: "It is impossible not to flourish in this land of sunshine and friendliness and, as one of our truly dear friends, you will receive an abundance of both." Nkrumah even offered Paul a professorship at the University of Ghana.

Perhaps encouraged by the loving response to his birthday, Paul began to take more interest in the world around him. As Dr. Ackner noted in one of his reports, "When he is depressed he loses all interest in the question of Negro rights and segregation in the USA, but when he becomes more cheerful he regains his interest."

Fortunately, Robeson's mood was on the upswing when word arrived from the U.S. Embassy that he needed to appear in person in order to update his passport. Without a valid passport, he could not renew his residence permit in England, which was also due to expire shortly. Essie arranged with friends to help bring Paul to the U.S. Embassy. The staff were British and sympathetic, and the American passport consul turned out to be a Robeson fan. The consul later reported to her superiors that "he appeared to be a very frail and subdued old man."

No unforeseen obstacles appeared, and the applications were quickly filled out and filed. Everyone breathed a sigh of relief. The Robesons went home to await the new passports.

Passport Problems—Again

No passports arrived. After six weeks, Essie learned that the State Department had decided to invoke a section of the Subversive Activities Control Act that denied the right of any member of a communist organization to apply for a passport. And the FBI had continued to keep Robeson on its list of Key Figures and Top Functionaries (of the Communist Party, that is).

The Robesons were told that in order to receive their passports, they had to submit sworn statements indicating whether they were or were not members of the party. A furious Essie dashed off to the embassy and deliberately created a scene, calling the requirement "sheer harassment." Everybody knew perfectly well, she angrily announced, that they were not party members, and she herself immediately swore an affidavit to that effect.

Paul was another matter. He'd always refused to sign any such affidavit, seeing it as an intolerable abridgement of his constitutional right to belong to any legal political party he chose. And he now refused again.

A frantic Essie hit on a clever strategy. She enlisted two of Paul's closest political friends, both party members, to write letters strongly urging him to sign the affidavit. One of them argued that Paul had done his share, that his "long, heroic and successful fight for a passport" had made travel possible "for hundreds of people." The struggle had now moved to a different level: to the right of *admitted* members of the party to obtain passports and to travel. Paul finally agreed to sign, and new passports quickly arrived.

Despite that success, Robeson's spirits again began to sink. He talked of his condition as "hopeless." Given the repetitive ups and downs, he said he held out no hope of recovery and expected simply "to wither away." The return of the Rosens in the summer of 1962 briefly revived him, but when they left he sank to another low and had to return to the Priory.

So it went for the next six months: periods of apathetic hopelessness alternating with brief improvement. In an effort to cheer him up, the tireless, remarkable Essie started planning far in advance to ensure a massive response for Paul's sixty-fifth birthday. She not only sent out a ton of mail soliciting greetings, but even outlined the sentiments she wanted people to stress: "Thank him for his example and courage and integrity during a very tough period." Paul, who had always avoided any crass bid for attention, would have been appalled at Essie's tactics.

But they worked. Paul received an avalanche of good wishes on his birthday. Yet if Essie expected gratitude, she was in for a shock. The more Paul read of the congratulatory letters, the angrier he got. "People are expecting too much from me again!" he started to shout. "They don't understand. I'll never sing again, never return again, never see any of them again. . . . I'll never be well. . . . I'll just sit in a corner . . . until maybe some sympathetic understanding doctor will give me something." Essie sighed. Essie protested. Essie kept right on going.

The next hurdle came from the press. By mid-1963, more than two years since Paul's breakdown in Moscow, rumors once more began to spread that he was disillusioned with the Soviet Union. A fake two-part article appeared under Paul's name in a fly-by-night sheet called the *National Insider* in which he "rejected" Soviet-style communism. The article was reprinted elsewhere, including in the prestigious French paper *Le Figaro.* With input from political friends, Essie sent off a strong counter-statement in which she denounced the original article as "pure fabrication." She stated that "there has been no interruption in [Paul's] warm friendship and close contact with our Soviet and Socialist friends."

When a posse of reporters descended on the Priory to get a statement from Paul—practically camping out around the place—the institution blocked access.

A New Clinic . . . and Home Again

To stop people from trying to pester Paul and from complaining about the Priory, Essie decided to make a shift in Paul's medical treatment. She visited the famed Buch Clinic in East Berlin. (At that time the city was divided by the Berlin Wall, with one part in East Germany, under Soviet influence, and the other in West Germany, under U.S. influence.) She was particularly impressed with Dr. Alfred Katzenstein, an American-trained clinical psychologist who'd served with the U.S. Army during World War II and had experience dealing with survivors of the Nazi concentration camps.

To slip Paul past the reporters at the Priory, Essie devised a series of deceptive ruses that gave famous mystery writer Agatha Christie a run for her money. The elaborate plan involved friends removing Essie's traveling luggage and overcoat from the Robesons' flat under the noses of reporters, while another friend sneaked Paul—who crouched on the floor of a car—out of the Priory grounds for a speedy drive to the airport, where the Robesons boarded a Polish flight to East Berlin.

Essie's plan had worked. Paul had been successfully spirited away, and the press left empty-handed.

At the Buch Clinic, Dr. Katzenstein found Robeson "completely without initiative"—his depressive moods "very low," his up moods "not high enough to be called manic." Essie reported home that coming to the Buch Clinic had "turned out to be a very fine move." However, she hid the bad news the Buch doctors had given her about her own health: her recurring cancer was terminal. Determined to live out what remained of her life at full tilt—as she always had—she told no one of the diagnosis and explained her own illness as flu or exhaustion. Once out of bed, she maintained a full schedule, even putting together a seminar at Berlin's Humboldt University on "The Negro and the USA."

Essie encouraged Paul to believe that they were both on the road to complete recovery. And, for a time after shifting to the Buch Clinic, Paul did show a marked improvement. Katzenstein even took him occasionally to feed the ducks in the park, on supervised outings to the zoo, or for brief visits to the Soviet-German House of Culture. A few expeditions were even more elaborate, including a trip downtown to be measured for a new overcoat or to take tea at the Soviet ambassador's residence.

On Thanksgiving Paul and Essie went to dinner at the home of a Black American singer named Aubrey Pankey, who'd moved to East Berlin. Years later Pankey's wife Kay recalled her shock on opening the door to the Robesons and seeing "a tall, gaunt, thin man; he was all eyes. My heart just went out."

The other guest that day was the well-regarded Black cartoonist Ollie Harrington, who was equally stunned at the sight of Robeson: "I'd never seen such a change in a man." The warm and witty Harrington decided to try and break through to Paul, so he "started to tell anecdotes we used in our 'special times' back in Harlem, tales about 'the stupidity of Charley' alternating with 'the ridiculous reaction of the Brothers.'"

Robeson slowly responded. His eyes gradually came alive, and he even laughed out loud a few times. On his way out the door, already lapsing back into melancholy, Paul impulsively grabbed Ollie's hand. "Thank you, thank you," he said over and over again.

Heading into another down cycle, Paul kept repeating that "I just can't make it any more . . . I'm too tired . . . I haven't got the energy." Essie tried to reassure him that he'd done his share, that nobody expected more from him, that everyone would understand if he simply announced that he was retiring from public life. Paul said he agreed—and went right on worrying. His father had trained him to believe that he must always do more and better. He could never quite believe that he'd done enough to allow him to retire with honor from the field.

At the same time, Robeson knew he didn't have the energy for any real involvement. He told Essie for the first time that as far back as 1956, following his prostate surgery, he'd never really felt mended. Now and then, he said, he could make "a supreme effort"—like playing *Othello* in Stratford in 1959, or the trip to Australia in 1960—though only with "great fear and worry." During the run of *Othello*, he confessed, "every perfor-mance was an ordeal."

Robeson's chief concern was that he couldn't rejoin the Black struggle in some significant way. He couldn't give up the hope that the new generation of Black activists would make some gesture, some request for his help. Perhaps, he thought, if I were home, more readily available . . . perhaps then. . . .

Essie told him that *he* had to make the decision about re-turning to the States, about what he wanted to do and where he wanted to go. She drew up a list for him of the possible places they could live, with the pros and cons of each. Finally, one morning in December 1963, Paul firmly said that he did want to go home, back to the States, back to his people.

They had several more go-rounds, but Paul, though enfee-bled, held to his decision. "This is what he seems to want," Essie reported to the family. "I know your welcome, and your concern will warm his heart, and relax him very much. He knows you won't expect him to DO anything, just BE."

Dr. Katzenstein and the Buch staff agreed that taking Paul back to the United States was the right decision. "There is no way of knowing," the doctor told Essie, "if he stayed longer whether he would improve more." He hoped Robeson "would find a peaceful home."

And so it was that on December 17, 1963, Paul and Essie flew to London. Five days later they boarded a jet for New York.

Chapter 14

FALLING SILENT
AT LAST

A "MUTED RETURN" IS HOW THE *NEW YORK POST* described the Robesons' arrival in New York. While reporters milled about the terminal in expectation of a press conference, Paul and Essie rapidly disappeared into a waiting car. The *New York Times* featured Robeson's return on the front page, describing him as "much thinner and not his old vociferous self." A separate *Times* profile recounting Robeson's history carried the headline DISILLUSIONED NATIVE SON.

The *Herald Tribune* went for a full-scale frontal assault. A lead editorial described Robeson as having "run away" when the civil rights struggle "got rough": "He abandoned the battle, as well as his country, to indulge a juvenile's taste for Marxist idealism, leaving it to others to stay at home to fight the war for civil rights. . . . Now that the back of the opposition to civil rights has been broken, Robeson returns anxious to jump on the bandwagon. . . . His countrymen have proved that they can manage without him." The wording could hardly have been more hurtful. It fueled Robeson's own worst nightmare—that he'd lost touch with the Black struggle and that his earlier contributions to it would be forgotten.

"The Time Is Now"

Robeson could do little about those who falsified his past accomplishments and gloated over his current disability. With minimal energy, constantly fearful of a relapse, he could neither give interviews nor face a formal press conference. Fortunately, he was shielded from most of the negative publicity and surrounded by people who had never ceased to regard him as a hero.

"Home" alternated between his sister Marian's house in Philadelphia and the apartment he shared with Essie in New York's Jumel Terrace. Only a few old and trusted friends, like the Rosens, were allowed to visit. Paul Jr., who had married and now had two young children, would come by nearly every morning before going to his job as a translator for technical journals. The two grandchildren were a particular source of pleasure—as Essie put it, "so gay and healthy and normal and busy and interested and interesting." By June 1964 Robeson was able to go with Paul Jr. to a baseball game. By then, he had put on thirty pounds and was near his normal weight of 250.

"Paul is so much better," Essie wrote a friend, "but he still says and feels he isn't," and still frets constantly that "people will not understand his idleness." He'd been through so many years of ups and downs that he was naturally cautious about the improvement in his health, but he did have more energy and was more interested in his surroundings. He was even, now and then, able to talk tentatively about becoming more active.

"He is now PLANNING, no less," Essie told the Rosens. "On a low level, but never mind." By late August, Robeson felt well enough to issue a brief public statement. For the time being, he wrote, he was unable to resume public life but he wanted it known that "I am, of course, deeply involved with the great upsurge of our people. Like all of you, my heart has been filled with admiration for the many thousands of Negro Freedom Fighters and their white associates who are waging the battle for civil rights throughout the country, and especially in the South."

He took pride in pointing out that when he'd written in *Here I Stand* in 1958, "The time is now," some people had thought "that perhaps my watch was fast (and maybe it was a little), but most of us seem to be running on the same time—now." He was pleased, too, that the call he'd sounded for unified action and mass militancy among Black people was no longer deemed "too radical." Most of them, he wrote, had come to agree with his 1949 Paris statement calling upon them to turn away from foreign wars and to save their strength for the struggle at home. "It was good," he said, "to see all these transformations."

Emboldened, Robeson took a few more steps forward. When the gifted playwright Lorraine Hansberry, who'd earlier worked with Robeson on the paper *Freedom*, died of cancer tragically young at thirty-four, Robeson not only appeared at her funeral service—despite a blizzard—but also delivered a eulogy that he'd written in advance. He paid tribute to Hansberry's "feeling and knowledge of the history of our people . . . remarkable in one so young," and reminded the crowd that she "bids us to keep our heads high and to hold on to our strength and power—to soar like the Eagle in the air."

At the Hansberry funeral, militant Black activist Malcolm X sent word that he would very much like to meet Robeson, whom he had already praised for his "brilliant stand" in a public speech. Robeson felt no kinship with the Black Muslim movement, with its emphasis on separatism, the confinement of women, and the prime importance of Black businesses. But for Malcolm himself he felt strong admiration. It was decided that day at Hansberry's funeral to put off the meeting of the two men to a later date. A month later, Malcolm X was assassinated.

Into the World Again

With the approach of Robeson's sixty-seventh birthday, the editors of *Freedomways*, a militant new Black magazine, asked if they could use the occasion to stage a "salute" to him that might also be a moneymaker for the magazine. Robeson gave the go-ahead, and the planning began. Among the sixty or so people who responded with enthusiasm were writer James Baldwin; actor Ossie Davis; musicians Dizzy Gillespie, John Coltrane, and Pete Seeger; scientist Linus Pauling; and progressive journalist I.F. Stone.

On the night of April 22, 1965, more than two thousand people filled a hotel ballroom for a four-hour celebration. John Lewis, chair of the Student Nonviolent Coordinating Committee (and later a member of the U.S. House of Representatives), delivered the keynote speech. His warm words rang out with comradely devotion: "We of SNCC are Paul Robeson's spiritual children. We too have rejected gradualism and moderation. We [too] are . . . being accused of radicalism, of communist infiltration." Bob Moses, a legendary SNCC leader, also showed up for the event and personally paid his respects to Robeson.

When Robeson took the podium, a near pandemonium of cheers, waves, and tears filled the room. Deeply moved, Robeson stuck to his prepared text, sounding many of the themes that had been central to his life: art as the reflection of "a common humanity"; the "great variety" in combination with "the universality" of human experience; the "oneness of many of the people in our contemporary world"; the importance of letting people "decide for themselves" between the contending systems of social organization.

He expressed, too, his pleasure that many of the "newly emancipated nations of Asia and Africa" were moving in the direction of a socialist arrangement, and that the struggle for the liberation of Black people in the United States was finding and building "a living connection—deeper and stronger—between the Negro people and the great masses of white Americans, who are indeed our natural allies in the struggle for democracy."

It was a memorable night. Indeed, the event had gone off so well that plans for a trip to California moved ahead. Careful advance arrangements were made to safeguard Paul from excessive expectations, and the trip started out well enough.

At the Los Angeles airport terminal Paul and Essie were met by two Black left-wing activists assigned as bodyguards, but there were no incidents of any kind. The Robesons went directly to the home, in the Watts neighborhood, of an old friend connected to the National Negro Labor Council. They rested all that day and the next until the time came for the celebration in Robeson's honor at the First Unitarian Church, where he gave essentially the same speech he had at his tribute in New York. He also sang a few songs without accompaniment. "This is the first time," he told the adoring crowd, "I'm sort of playing around much with the singing, but I guess the voice is still around somewhere."

Essie thought it sounded better than that—"full, complete with overtones, and under very firm control." He "seems to feel very experimental," Essie wrote home to the family. "He wants to try things. I am keeping clear watch, so no one can push him, and that he gets rest." She made a particular point of seeing to it that none of the Communist Party people got anywhere near him.

She was equally alert when they went north to San Francisco, though Paul began to wake up feeling already tired—which was not a good omen. Essie herself had developed severe back pain; she already knew from her doctors, though she told no one, that the cancer had spread and that she had only a limited amount of time left. Unable to conceal her pain entirely, she told an alarmed Paul that the problem was "either kidney or bladder" and would not last.

The Robesons managed to attend the first of the events scheduled, but on June 4—the evening of a long-planned and elaborate "Salute to Paul Robeson" at the Jack Tar Hotel—both Paul and Essie were so sick that mere willpower could no longer continue to stand in for health. Unable to attend the salute, they made immediate plans to return to New York and cut short their planned ten-day stay in San Francisco.

Another Retreat

Having missed the grand event in San Francisco and come home early, Paul felt that he'd "let the folks down." Once home he slid quickly into depression. Moody, uncommunicative, uninterested in food or people or events, he sat around the apartment in pajamas. On the evening of June 10, Essie came upon Paul "holding scissors to his chest." He managed to inflict a superficial wound before she could, "with difficulty," get the scissors away from him. Later that same day Paul Jr. walked into the bedroom and found his father, his face blank with terror, holding a double-edged razor blade in his hand. He quickly took it from him.

Paul Jr. and Essie concluded that it was no longer possible to safely keep Paul at home. They consulted with his doctors, including Sam Rosen, and decided to admit him to Gracie Square Hospital, a psychiatric facility. The recent high hopes for a continuing return to health had suddenly turned to ashes.

Robeson was assigned special nurses around the clock and put in a private room. For the first few days the doctors found him "polite" and able to respond to questions appropriately. He refused, though, to leave his room, and showed occasional "confusion." (One night he packed up a suitcase and told the nurses that a car was waiting.) Still, his condition did not worsen, and after a three-week stay, the doctors decided to let him return to Jumel Terrace. He reluctantly agreed to schedule at least occasional appointments with a young psychiatrist named Ari Kiev for "monitoring."

Kiev was initially struck above all by Robeson's "great sadness." He clearly felt, according to Kiev, "unappreciated" by the current generation of Black activists. Kiev saw Robeson overall as an "innocent" in the best sense: not naive but "pure"; he was motivated by compassion, not ego. Robeson was, according to Kiev, a man "fundamentally puzzled" at how his humane instincts and vision had run aground.

Kiev was saying what DuBois had said earlier: "The only thing wrong with Robeson is having too great faith in human beings." In place of the affirmation Robeson had grown used to receiving from his audiences, the government had branded and isolated him. The wonder to Kiev was not that Robeson had broken down under the punishment, but that he had not broken down sooner. The psychiatrist prescribed medication to treat Robeson's depression, and during the two months he saw him, Kiev felt that the patient became "more communicative and cheerful."

It was now Essie's turn on the grimly alternating cycle. Her pain finally became so great that she reluctantly yielded to it and was hospitalized for a series of treatments. Paul Jr. rightfully felt that his father would do poorly if left alone at Jumel Terrace, so Helen and Sam Rosen took Paul to their summer house outside of Peekskill.

There Robeson seemed to revive almost immediately. When Helen decided on a swim one day, Paul walked down to the pond with her. Then he suddenly walked over to the twelve-foot-high dam, which had steps going down into the pond. He put his foot on the top step, looked over at Helen, and then, with "a devilish laugh," as she later recalled, put his foot down on the next step. Paul couldn't swim, and Helen became immediately alarmed. Trying to stay calm, she walked over casually and smilingly suggested that he not get his shoes and his nice suit wet. She took his arm, and he let her guide him back to the grass.

She and Paul Jr. consulted with Ari Kiev, who advised a return to Gracie Square. Robeson offered no resistance, saying, "I'll do whatever you think best." On the day of his admission, August 7, 1965, Kiev wrote on Robeson's chart "Depression, suicidal thoughts and agitation in setting of wife's admission to hospital."

Three days later, Essie underwent surgery. Invasive cancer was found throughout her body, and the doctors said she had only a short time to live. Paul wasn't told, yet his own depression steadily deepened to the point where one doctor described him as "almost catatonic." By mid-August he'd developed bacterial double pneumonia. His temperature shot up to 105 degrees, and he was transferred to the superior medical facilities at University Hospital (now Tisch Hospital at NYU Langone Health). That decision saved his life. Although the pneumonia was successfully treated, his mental health diagnosis of "psychosis" did not change.

Paul and Essie were released from their hospitals within days of each other. Essie was dying, and Paul was uncertainly involved with life. Two women friends moved in to take care of them. Essie lay in bed desperately ill, while Paul, in his own solitude, brooding and melancholy, passed unpredictably from room to room.

Paul Jr. was in constant attendance. One day he heard the front door slam. Racing to the door, he discovered his father was gone. He and a friend unsuccessfully scoured the neighborhood, then called the police. Early the next morning Robeson was found lying in a clump of bushes a few blocks from Jumel Terrace. He had no recollection of what had happened to him. After treatment for lacerations and bruises, it was decided that he should be taken to his sister Marian's house in Philadelphia. Her warmth and concern, Paul's caretakers rightly concluded, would prove the best possible medicine.

Essie was near death and in severe discomfort. Her unquiet, tenacious spirit finally stilled on December 12, when she died two days before her seventieth birthday. Paul was told, but he said nothing in response to the news. Nor was he able to attend the small, private funeral.

Last Days with Marian

Marian Robeson Forsythe, Paul's sister, was a seventy-one-year-old widow and retired schoolteacher. She lived in an unpretentious house on Walnut Street in Philadelphia where she cared for her adult daughter Paulina, who'd been withdrawn and often mute since childhood. Marian, who'd always worshipped her younger brother, took on the additional responsibility of caring for him. The two had always felt entirely comfortable with each other, and Marian was totally devoted to his well-being. An intensely private person, Marian was ideally equipped to protect Paul from any unwanted intrusion.

Robeson had always taken for granted that others would provide for his practical daily needs, but now he could no longer reward them with warmth and charm. He stayed very much to himself, talking little, though apparently understanding what was said to him. On one of his unaccountably "good days" he might accompany Marian on an errand, or take a walk with her in the neighborhood. On an especially good day he would go with her to see a film. His was essentially the life of a cherished—though haunted—invalid. Marian attended to his every need, and she greeted every sign of sociability with hopeful delight.

Occasionally word would arrive of some mention of Robeson in the outer world. In 1967 *Who's Who in American History* finally included his biography. And from Rutgers University came word, after fifty years of omission, that he'd been nominated for the National Football Hall of Fame. Told the news, Robeson smiled and shrugged.

As the days and years of being out of the public eye lengthened, the world inexorably changed. In 1968 sectors of the white working class rallied to the racist presidential campaign of George Wallace, who received 10 million votes. SNCC declined into warring sects and then disappeared. And Robeson became a faded memory to one generation, an unknown name to the next. People over forty wondered what had ever become of him (the rumor spread that he'd gone into self-exile in Russia). Many people under forty had no idea that he'd ever existed.

Still, old devotions held firm in some quarters. On Robeson's seventieth birthday, an evening of music, poetry, and drama was put on in his honor in London. The participants included a number of old friends and colleagues, including Bruno Raikin, Peggy Ashcroft, Sybil Thorndike, and Flora Robson. Speaking for the new generation, South African Oliver Tambo—who would one day serve in exile as leader of the militant African National Congress—wrote in honor of "a universal idol and a friend dear to all who know him or have only heard his priceless voice."

A few years later, in 1972, Robeson even received a number of awards. He was in the first group of people elevated into the Theater Hall of Fame, *Sports Illustrated* carried a story about his athletic prowess, and *Ebony* named him among the "10 Greats of Black History."

The number of people who wanted to visit Robeson was always greater than the number who were allowed to do so. A few people, like Helen and Sam Rosen, had free access, limited by their own sense of appropriateness and a last-minute check to be sure he was up to seeing them. But Marian and Paul Jr. barred visits from mere acquaintances. As for the idly curious, they were held fiercely at bay.

The Rosens went down to Philadelphia about once a month. They often found Paul "sort of sleepy," but on his better days he would talk theater or (with Sam) football. His doctors, unlike some of his friends, did not mistake the temporary improvement of "a good day" for any prospect of permanent rehabilitation. They made it clear that he would not recover. He could only be made comfortable.

Marian and Paul Jr. never discouraged Robeson's occasional

interest in the outside world. However, aware of how prone he was to blame himself for "not doing more," they avoided encouraging him to "try harder," or to hold out hope that he might yet make a significant public contribution. Their aim was to do nothing to disturb a daily routine that most of the time produced the appearance of serenity, minimized mood swings, and made heroic medical interventions unnecessary.

Robeson's seventy-fifth birthday in April 1973 became the first real occasion to celebrate his lifetime accomplishments. He was unable to attend the event at Carnegie Hall, but he did send a brief taped message to the large gathering. Tumultuous applause greeted a multimedia scripted show that featured live actors interspersed with recordings, slides, and movies depicting highlights from Robeson's career.

The former U.S. attorney general Ramsey Clark spoke of Robeson embodying "the grace and beauty" that America was "afraid of." Pete Seeger got the crowd singing along with him on "Freiheit," a song from the Spanish Civil War that Robeson had often performed. Dolores Huerta, vice president of the United Farm Workers, elicited roars of "Viva Robeson!" when she linked his name to the cause of migrant farm laborers. Mayor Richard G. Hatcher of Gary, Indiana, called Robeson "our own black prince and prophet." And, crucially, Coretta Scott King, widow of Martin Luther King Jr., spoke of Robeson's having been "buried alive" because, earlier than her husband, he had "tapped the same wells of latent militancy."

A large number of notables from the Black community attended the event, and an even larger number sent tributes. Andrew Young wrote from the House of Representatives to thank

Robeson for his "beautiful life" and to say that, had Robeson not "kept alive a legacy of hope through some of the darkest days of our history . . . our accomplishments in the '60s would not have been possible." That same theme was picked up and broadened by a host of leaders from Third World countries: Julius K. Nyerere, president of Tanzania; Prime Minister Michael Manley of Jamaica; Cheddi Jagan of Guyana; Errol Barrow of Barbados; and the president of Zambia, Kenneth Kaunda. Sounding a more personal note, India's Indira Gandhi recalled "the wonder" on meeting him "of finding such gentleness in such a powerful frame."

A little more than two years later, Robeson was hospitalized with what was thought to be a mild stroke. To his cardiologist's surprise, there was "an abrupt onset of weakness"—and then a final stroke. Robeson was gone. A hospital spokesperson announced to the press that the cause of death was "complications arising from severe cerebral vascular disorder."

Condolences came in from around the world. After decades of harassing Robeson, the white press now tipped its hat to "a great American"—while at the same time downplaying the racism that had been central to his persecution. Such articles ignored the continuing inability of white America to tolerate a Black maverick who refused to bend.

The Black press made no such mistake. One paper, in a paroxysm of grief, splashed GOODBYE PAUL! on its front page. Another paid tribute to this "Gulliver among the Lilliputians"—a giant among those much smaller than he.

A cold rain fell all day outside Mother A.M.E. Zion Church in Harlem on January 27, 1976. Despite the rain, thousands

An Amsterdam News Tribute To A Man!

Goodbye Paul!

"Let's Be Grateful That We Lived In His Time!"

By L. CLAYTON JONES

One watches with restrained anger as a nation of hypocrites grudgingly acknowledges the passing of a twentieth century phenomenon. Paul Robeson, All American athlete, Shakespearean actor, basso profundo, linguist, scholar, lawyer, activist.

He was all these things and more.

I suspect, however, that the essential Paul Robeson is to be found in the uses to which he put his massive intellect. At bottom, he was an intellectual activist possessed of impeccable academic credentials.

Paul Robeson, 1898–1976

A portion of Paul Robeson's obituary in the New York Amsterdam News, one of the city's largest Black newspapers

of people, mostly Black, gathered on the sidewalks and slowly moved inside the historic Black church: leftists of several generations and philosophies, theater people and trade unionists, communists and conservatives, dear friends, old adversaries, complete strangers. Those in attendance included hundreds of Harlem's so-called ordinary people along with a variety of well-known figures: A. Philip Randolph, Bayard Rustin, the Rosens, Harry Belafonte, Uta Hagen, Betty Shabazz (widow of

A memorial poster of Paul Robeson, created by Raphael Romero of the Wilfred Owen Brigade in San Francisco

Malcolm X), Steve Nelson of the Abraham Lincoln Brigade, and Harry Winston, national chair of the Communist Party USA. As they filed in, Robeson's voice came out over the loudspeakers, singing the spirituals and songs most closely connected to him. His closed casket at the foot of the pulpit was draped in black, covered with red roses.

Bishop J. Clinton Hoggard, a boyhood friend, delivered the eulogy. He used a verse from Galatians—"Henceforth, let no man trouble me"—to recount the history of a man who had tried to live "with dignity" and who, for his persistence, "bore on his body marks of vengeance." Hoggard ended by paraphrasing a line Robeson used to sing at the close of the song "Joe Hill": "Don't mourn for me, but live for freedom's cause."

A Prisoner's Poetic Tribute

Amid the tributes to Paul Robeson that filled newspapers, magazines, and airwaves after his death, a Black prisoner in a penitentiary in Marion, Illinois, wrote a poem to express his sense of loss—and also his sense of what Robeson had given him:

PAUL ROBESON

They knocked the leaves
  From his limbs,
The bark
  From his
    Tree
But his roots
  were
    so deep
That they are
  a part of me.[12]

ACKNOWLEDGMENTS

When I decided the moment was ripe to do a young adult version of my original biography of Paul Robeson, Ellen Adler responded with immediate, enthusiastic encouragement; and as the book took shape, she remained an active partner in the process, providing me (as always in the past) with a large number of valuable suggestions. So, too, has Rebeca Stefoff, whose knowledge of young adult readers is unsurpassed. She has overseen my conversion of the original biography with immense graciousness and tact, filling in helpful sidebars when needed and gently aiding me in reworking my prose to make it responsive to a new generation. My thanks to Jay Gupta for his extensive photo research (not to mention his indulgence of my lack of digital skills); and also to the ever-reliable Maury Botton, who as always before, made the production process move like clockwork. Finally, I want to thank Jason Reynolds for his wonderfully warm and pointed foreword.

For Further Information on Paul Robeson

WEBSITES

"What Paul Robeson Said"
www.smithsonianmag.com/history/what-paul-robeson-said-77742433/
From *Smithsonianmag.com*, a close look at Paul Robeson's political activism and controversy, beginning with his misquoted speech at the 1949 Paris Peace Conference.

"Paul Robeson: Here I Stand"
www.pbs.org/wnet/americanmasters/paul-robeson-about-the-actor/66/
This page for the PBS episode on Robeson from its *American Masters* series features a brief biography and a career timeline. The two-hour *American Masters* documentary film about Robeson, made in 1999, is available from many libraries and from multiple commercial sources on videotape and digital media.

Paul Robeson Home
www.nps.gov/nr/travel/civilrights/ny1.htm
The Paul Robeson Residence in New York City has been preserved by the National Park Service as part of its We Shall Overcome: Historic Places of the Civil Rights Movement. This Park Service page offers a brief biography of Robeson.

Paul Robeson Cultural Center, Rutgers University
prcc.rutgers.edu/about-us-2/paul-robeson/
The Paul Robeson Cultural Center on the campus where Robeson went to college honors his legacy as an activist and an artist. This website includes a brief biography.

SELECTED PERFORMANCES AND APPEARANCES TO VIEW
ONLINE (ALL AVAILABLE AS OF AUGUST 2020)

Paul Robeson Sings "Ol' Man River" in *Show Boat*
www.youtube.com/watch?v=eh9WayN7R-s

Paul Robeson Sings to Scottish Miners, 1949
www.youtube.com/watch?v=B0bezsMVU7c

The Tallest Tree, Parts 1 and 2 (documentary film)
www.youtube.com/watch?v=uPRS-GX9n-A
www.youtube.com/watch?v=fgCtDoFz7TA

Remembering the Overlooked Life of Eslanda Robeson, Wife of Civil
Rights Icon Paul Robeson (from *Democracy Now!*)
www.youtube.com/watch?v=K3Ezymqbw-M

Paul Robeson's Music and Movies

SELECTED RECORDINGS

The following are some of the albums released during Paul Robeson's lifetime. Many additional collections of his recordings have been released or rereleased in recent years.

Ballad for Americans, Victor, 1940

Songs of Free Men, Columbia Masterworks, 1943

Spirituals, Columbia Masterworks, 1945

Here Comes the Showboat, Columbia, 1946

A Robeson Recital of Popular Favorites, Columbia Masterworks, 1947

I Came to Sing, International Union of Mine, Mill, and Smelters Workers Union, 1952

Robeson Sings, Othello Records, 1953

Paul Robeson Sings, Philips, 1956

Emperor of Song!, His Master's Voice, 1957

Robeson, Amadeo, 1958

Favorite Songs, Monitor Records, 1959

"Encore, Robeson!" Paul Robeson Favorites, Volume Two, Monitor Records, 1960

At Carnegie Hall, Vanguard, 1960

Robeson, Verve Records, 1960

Paul Robeson Recital, Supraphon, 1961

Paul Robeson Sings Negro Spirituals, Concert Hall, 1961

Paul Robeson, Super Majestic, 1965

Ballad for Americans, Carnegie Hall Concert, Volume Two, Vanguard, 1965

The Greatness of Paul Robeson, CBS, 1965

Spirituals, CBS, 1968

In Live Performance, Columbia Masterworks, 1970

Paul Robeson, World Record Club, 1971

A Portrait of Paul Robeson, His Master's Voice, 1975

MOVIES

Paul Robeson acted in or narrated the films listed here. Many are now available from libraries or commercial sources. For example, the Criterion Collection offers the four-disc DVD set *Paul Robeson: Portraits of the Artist*, which includes the films *Body and Soul, Borderline, The Emperor Jones, Sanders of the River, Jericho, The Proud Valley*, and *Native Land*, as well as the 1979 short documentary film *Paul Robeson: Tribute to an Artist*, narrated by Sidney Poitier.

Body and Soul, 1925

Camille, 1926

Borderline, 1930

The Emperor Jones, 1933

Sanders of the River, 1935

Show Boat, 1936

Song of Freedom, 1936

Big Fella, 1937

King Solomon's Mines, 1937

My Song Goes Forth, 1937

Jericho (also known as *Dark Sands*), 1937

Canciones de Madrid (Songs of Madrid, documentary), 1938

The Proud Valley, 1940

Tales of Manhattan, 1942

Native Land (narrator), 1942

Das Lied der Ströme (The Song of the Rivers, narrator), 1954

Sources

A NOTE ON THE SOURCES FOR THIS BOOK

Paul Robeson: No One Can Silence Me is based on the definitive biography of Paul Robeson by Martin Duberman, which was published in 1989 (*Paul Robeson: A Biography*, Knopf). Like the original biography, *Paul Robeson: No One Can Silence Me* is based almost entirely on unpublished manuscript sources. Duberman is the only scholar ever given unimpeded access to the vast Robeson Family Archives, now housed at the Moorland-Spingarn Research Center at Howard University. In addition, Duberman read through the material in the previously closed Paul Robeson Archive at the Akademie der Künste in Germany, and also drew upon the unpublished papers of some 60 Robeson friends and colleagues housed in 28 manuscript libraries scattered across the country. He conducted personal interviews with 132 Robeson friends and associates. Duberman donated all of the tape recordings of those interviews to the Moorland-Spingarn Research Center. Finally, under the Freedom of Information Act (FOIA), he brought a formal lawsuit against the FBI in order to extract additional material from the bureau's long-standing surveillance files on Robeson. For more extensive information on the source material Duberman used to write this biography, please consult the original biography, *Paul Robeson: A Biography* (reprinted by The New Press, 1995), 557–804.

Introduction: Performance and Protest

xvii **"I have made a lifelong habit"** *Chicago Defender*, February 21, 1942.

xviii **"with stronger feeling"** *Kansas City Times*, February 18, 1942.

xviii **"for the stand you took"** Letter from Lucile Bluford to Paul Robeson, February 21, 1942.

xx **"the leader of the colored race in America"** Rutgers University 1919 "Class Prophecy."

Chapter 1: A Boy's Balancing Act

4 **"a hint of servility"** Paul Robeson, "From My Father's Parsonage," *Sunday Sun* (London), January 13, 1929.

6 **"the oppressing hand"** Paul Robeson, *Here I Stand* (Beacon Press, 1971), 20.

6 **Paul knew that he'd had what he later called** Marie Seton, *Paul Robeson* (Dennis Dobson, 1958), cut from the published book at Robeson's request.

6 **"I get a little mad, man, get a little angry"** Public remarks by Paul Robeson in Australia in 1960, tape courtesy of Lloyd L. Davies.

9 **"the virtues of self-reliance, self-respect"** Paul Robeson's valedictory speech, Robeson Archives, also printed in the *Daily Targum* (Rutgers University), June 1919.

10 **"where an injury to the meanest citizen"** Ibid.

10 **He took the lead in "profound discussions"** Interview with Sadie Goode Davenport Shelton and her son Robert Davenport, March 26, 1985.

Chapter 2: New Roles in Private and Public Life

14 **she had admired Paul at a distance** Essie Robeson, autobiographical manuscript, in Robeson Archives.

14 **"He let things happen"** Interview with Henry A. Murray, February 6, 1985.

15 **would hold him back less in theater** Essie Robeson, autobiographical manuscript, in Robeson Archives.

16 **he could never have entered "any profession where"** Paul Robeson, "From My Father's Parsonage," *Sunday Sun* (London), January 13, 1929.

17 **The New York Times hailed his performance** *New York Times,* May 7, 1924.

17 **the New York Evening Graphic declared** *New York Evening Graphic,* December 16, 1924.

18 **Paul later said that he'd gone onstage** Interview with Paul Robeson, *The Star* (London), December 28, 1929.

18 **"superbly embodied and fully comprehended"** *The Sun* (New York), May 16, 1924.

22 **"destined to be the new American Caruso"** Edgar G. Brown, *New York Daily News,* April 25, 1925.

22 **He and Essie found an ideal flat** Essie Robeson diary, August 1925, in Robeson Archives.

22 **a "warm, friendly and unprejudiced" reception** Essie Robeson, autobiographical manuscript, in Robeson Archives.

24 **Ira Aldridge had seen the play and wrote to thank Paul** Letter to Paul Robeson from Miss Ira Aldridge, Robeson Archives.

Chapter 3: A Career Takes Flight

29 **He criticized Robeson's character Joe** *New York Amsterdam News,* October 3, 1928.

29 **During the yearlong London run of Show Boat** Letter from Essie Robeson to Otto Kahn, January 21, 1929, Princeton University Library.

31 **He was especially delighted when a Polish musician** *Musical Standard,* March 22, 1930.

Chapter 4: Drama On and Off the Stage

34 **Robeson had told a reporter that in London** Interview with Paul Robeson, Ceylon *Morning Leader,* September 13, 1929.

34 **"is not in accordance with our British hotel practice"** Marie Seton, *Paul Robeson* (Dennis Dobson, 1958), 50–52.

34 **"the influence of American race prejudice"** Interview with Paul Robeson, *New York State Contender*, October 28, 1929.

35 **At the start of rehearsals for *Othello*** Letter from Essie Robeson to Nellie Van Volkenburg, May 1930, Labadie Collection, University of Michigan, Browne: Van Volkenburg.

35 **Poor Paul," she added, "is lost"** Essie Robeson diary, April 15–16, 1930.

35 **"There are other people on the stage besides yourself"** Interview with Peggy Ashcroft, September 9, 1982.

35 **"Of course I do not mind!"** *Daily Sketch*, May 21, 1930.

36 **They made Paul feel so skittish** *New York Times*, January 16, 1944.

37 **Paul was "wild with nerves"** Essie Robeson diary, May 19–20, 1930.

37 **Robeson's reviews ran the gamut** *Daily Mail*, May 20, 1930.

37 **to "prosaic"** *News of the World*, May 25, 1930.

37 **and "disappointing"** *Daily News*, May 20, 1930.

37 **A few of the critics struck an unmistakably racist note** *Country Life*, May 31, 1920.

38 **"the audience would get rough"** *New York Times*, May 22, 1930.

38 **"He knows what would happen and so do the rest of us"** *Times Enterprise* (Thomasville, GA), May 27, 1930.

38 **Essie accused him of being "a smooth one"** Essie Robeson diary, October 1930.

39 **"Let's hope all will come out right"** Letter from Paul Robeson to Essie Robeson, September 29, 1930, Robeson Archives.

39 **She characterized it in her diary as "cold, mean, vindictive"** Essie Robeson diary, October 1930.

39 **"I have been terribly ill with nerves"** Letter from Essie Robeson to Carl Van Vechten and Fania Marinoff, December 19, 1930, Beinecke Library, Yale University: Van Vechten.

40 **"He can't seem to make up his mind"** Essie Robeson diary, November 8, 1931.

40 **"the most beautifully blended musical show"** Brooks Atkinson, *New York Times*, May 20, 1932.

41 **"I desire above all things to maintain my personal dignity"** *Sunday News*, June 26, 1932.

41 **She gloried in the rumors that Paul** Essie Robeson diary, July 11, 1932.

42 **As late as 1950, she confessed in a letter to Larry Brown** Letter from Yolande Jackson to Larry Brown, n.d., New York Public Library, Schomburg Collection: Brown.

44 **A number of Black intellectuals and newspapers criticized Robeson** *Philadelphia Tribune*, November 2, 1933.

45 **"the plantation type of Negro"** *Film Weekly*, September 1, 1933.

Chapter 5: Discovering Africa

47 **"Why should we copy something that's inferior?"** *Film Weekly*, September 1, 1933.

48 **"I am essentially an artist and a cosmopolitan"** Interview with Paul Robeson in *Tit-Bits*, May 27, 1933.

48 **As time went on, Robeson's study of phonetics** Paul Robeson, "The Culture of the Negro," *The Spectator*, June 15, 1934.

49 **could become "a self-respecting"** Paul Robeson notes, 1934, Robeson Archives.

50 **He considered it essential, above all** Ibid.

51 **"When we get through," she wrote to the Van Vechtens"** Letter from Essie Robeson to Carl Van Vechten and Fania Marinoff, April 5, 1934, Beinecke Library, Yale University: Van Vechten.

51 **"you have at last set your feet on the right road"** Letter from Zora Neale Hurston to Essie Robeson, April 18, 1934, Robeson Archives.

51 **He announced to the press** *The Spectator*, June 15, 1934.

52 **"the music of basic realities"** *Perth* (Australia) *Advertiser*, January 20, 1934.

52 **"the most retrograde [backward] step the world has seen"** *Jewish Transcript*, November 22, 1935.

53 **"I'm not kidding myself that I've really gotten a place in Western culture"** *The Observer*, July 29, 1934.

53 **The character Bosambo was presented** Thomas Cripps, "Paul Robeson and Black Identity in American Movies," *Massachusetts Review*, Summer 1970, 480.

54 **"a grand insight into our special English difficulties"** *Sunday Times* (London), April 7, 1935.

54 **"Here we have the pathetic spectacle"** Robert Stebbins, *New Theatre*, July 1935.

Chapter 6: Nazis, Communists—and Hollywood

59 **Paul—who spoke Russian fluently—explained that his chief interest** *Moscow Daily News*, December 24, 1934.

59 **To emphasize the point, he added** *The Observer* (London), April 28, 1935.

60 **"The people have gone mad over [Paul]"** Letter from Essie Robeson to Ma Goode, January 25, 1935, Robeson Archives.

61 **Robeson's favorite was *General Line*, the story of** *Picturegoer Weekly*, October 26, 1935.

61 **Paul told Eisenstein how deeply moved** Marie Seton, *Paul Robeson* (Dennis Dobson, 1958), 94–95.

62 **"Paul is extraordinarily happy these days"** Letter from Essie Robeson to Ma Goode, February 8, 1935, Robeson Archives.

64 **"we can all live happily and comfortably"** Letter from Essie Robeson to Hattie Bolling, December 12, 1935, Robeson Archives.

65 **"not only of great gentleness but of great command"** C.L.R. James, "Paul Robeson: Black Star," *Black World*, November 1970, 114.

66 **"He was a distinguished person"** Interview with C.L.R. James, November 1983.

66 **"For no one respects a man who does not respect himself"** Paul Robeson notes, 1936, Robeson Archives.

67 **Robeson insisted that he based nothing** Ibid.

68 **"maximizing both liberty and variety inside every human group"** Letter from Norman Leys to Leonard Barnes, June 11, 1935, copy to the Robesons, Robeson Archives.

68 **But he did not share their view** Paul Robeson notes, 1935, Robeson Archives.

70 **He once wrote that it was delusional** Paul Robeson notes, 1936, Robeson Archives.

72 **[But in truth] Africa was opened up** Robeson Archives.

73 **"Robeson is made to sing childish lyrics to dreary tunes"** *Pittsburgh Courier*, August 14, 1937.

73 **"This was Paul Robeson plus!"** Interview with Henry Wilcoxon, September 1982.

Chapter 7: The World Goes to War

77 **He made a point of visiting workers' homes** *Sunday Worker*, May 10, 1936.

78 **"I want to go to Spain"** Letter from Essie Robeson to William Patterson, March 22, 1928, Moorland-Spingarn Research Center, Howard University: Patterson.

78 **"Why need he go into the war area"** Essie Robeson, Spain, Robeson Archives.

79 **"When he talks, he talks passionately"** Nicolás Guillén interview, reprinted in translation by Katheryn Silver, *World Magazine*, July 24, 1976.

79 **he angrily denounced the "so- called democracies"** Ibid.

81 **"all the American Negro comrades who have come to fight and die for Spain"** Paul Robeson notes, 1938, "My Impressions of Spain."

82 **well-developed political sympathies** Paul Robeson, *Here I Stand* (Beacon Press, 1971), 53.

82 **"I have never met such courage"** Paul Robeson notes, "My Impressions of Spain," 1938, Robeson Archives.

83 **a film he now called "a total loss"** *Daily Record* (Chicago), February 28, 1939.

84 **"I am tired of playing Stepin Fetchit comics"** *Daily Telegraph*, November 1, 1938.

Chapter 8: Hero—and Traitor?

87 **He made it a point in his acceptance speech** Paul Robeson, "Notes on Speech at Hamilton College," Robeson Archives.

90 **moving "toward something resembling our own and Great Britain's democracy"** Quoted in Irving Howe and Lewis Coser, *The American Communist Party: A Critical History* (Da Capo Press, 1974), 431–33.

91 **"Given his well-documented abuses and prejudices"** Congressman Steve Cohen, press release, October 22, 2015.

93 **"He was available to you"** Interview with Howard "Stretch" Johnson, March 5, 1985.

93 **The majority of Black reviewers declared** *New York Amsterdam Star News*, August 15, 1942.

96 **"He didn't fall for praise"** Interviews with Uta Hagen, June 21–22, 1982, and September 28, 1984.

97 **"the applause and the bravos echoed"** *Newsweek*, November 1, 1943.

97 **definitely gave Robeson his due** Wolcott Gibbs, *New Yorker*, October 30, 1943.

97 **"the human presence was so big"** Interviews with Uta Hagen, June 21–22, 1982, and September 28, 1984.

99 **After the hearing** Interview with James Earl Jones, *New York Times*, January 31, 1982.

99 **She wondered if the powers that be in Hollywood** Fredi Washington, *People's Voice*, October 23, 1943.

100 **one of the few times Hagen ever saw Paul "lose his cool"** Interviews with Uta Hagen, June 21–22, 1982, and September 28, 1984.

Chapter 9: At the Peak of Fame

105 **The Peoria city council had recently passed a resolution** "Peoria Bans Robeson; He Vows to Sing," *Chicago Daily Tribune,* April 18, 1947, 1.

105 **"If Communism means pointing out to the people"** *Chicago Sun,* April 20, 1947.

110 **Two things, Robeson answered** Transcript of Paul Robeson testimony before the Senate Judiciary Committee, Robeson Archives.

110 **After the hearing** *The Afro-American,* June 10, 1948.

Chapter 10: "The Struggle" Hits Home

115 **all that he said was carefully reasoned** Valentine Elliott, in the June–August issue of *Makarere,* Makarere College, British East Africa.

116 **"people who have become very dear to me"** Letter from Paul Robeson to Helen Rosen, n.d. (March -April 1949), courtesy Rosen.

118 **"We shall not make war on the Soviet Union"** From a French transcript, translated by Alphaeus Hunton, Robeson Archives.

118 **"has raised our people to the full dignity of mankind"** Transcript of AP dispatch, Robeson Archives.

118 **the courtly, highly respected** A. Philip Randolph, quoted in Patrick S. Washburn, *A Question of Sedition: The Federal Government's Investigation of the Black Press During World War II* (Oxford University Press, 1986).

120 **"any conflict that our nation has with any other"** *New York Herald Tribune,* May 1, 1949, and many other places in the press, as well as distributed by the State Department.

120 **"There's a sort of unwritten law"** Interviews with Bayard Rustin, March 25 and April 20, 1983.

121 **At the heart of the agenda** Ibid.

122 **has not felt as Robeson expressed himself** *Carolina Times* (Durham, NC), April 30, 1949.

123 **Another Black editorial declared** *Columbia Record* (SC), May 2, 1949.

123 **"I say Paul Robeson speaks more for the real colored people"** Abner Berry, *New York Age*, May 21, 1949.

123 **"A certain sheep-like disposition"** *New York Amsterdam News*, May 21, 1949.

124 **"he doesn't get a dime for doing it"** Letter from Charles P. Howard to Roy Wilkins, May 26, 1949, Chicago Historical Society: Barnett.

125 **The editorial patronizingly suggested** *New York Times*, April 25, 1949.

127 **"I met Jewish people all over the place"** Amy Schechter, "Paul Robeson's Soviet Journey," *Soviet Russia Today*, August 1949.

129 **"I have seen how the Chinese are treated in San Francisco"** Ibid.

130 **"He read it, he knew it was true"** Multiple conversations with Paul Robeson Jr.

133 **"We do not want to die in vain any more"** Paul Robeson, transcript of speech, Robeson Archives.

135 **He left immediately for New York** *Hearings Regarding Communist Infiltration of Minority Groups*, July 13–18, 1949, U.S. Government Printing Office.

135 **"Mr. Robeson has attached himself"** *New York Times*, July 19, 1949.

135 **the *Amsterdam News*, hailed Robinson** *New York Amsterdam News*, July 23, 1949.

135 **Another Black newspaper** *The Afro-American*, July 19, 1949.

136 **there was "no argument between Jackie and me"** Statement released from CAA office by Paul Robeson, July 20, 1949.

136 **"he was sincerely trying to help his people"** Jackie Robinson, *I Never Had It Made* (Putnam's Sons, 1972), 98.

137 **A rash of activity immediately followed** From the privately printed *Eyewitness: Peekskill USA*, Westchester Committee for a Fair Inquiry into the Peekskill Violence.

139 **I'll be back with my friends in Peekskill!"** From a recording of Paul Robeson's speech at the Golden Gate Ballroom, Harlem, Robeson Archives.

141 **That same DA** *National Guardian*, September 19, 1949.

141 **"In the whole history of the United States"** Gilbert Ware, *William Hastie: Grace Under Pressure* (Oxford University Press, 1984), 228.

Chapter 11: The Fight for the Right to Travel

145 **"to run the world"** Paul Robeson speech transcript, October 5, 1950, Robeson Archives.

145 **She worked particularly hard** FBI Main 100-12304-255.

147 **The famous boxer Sugar Ray Robinson** *New York Herald Tribune*, January 3, 1951.

147 **More hurtful still** Walter White, "The Strange Case of Paul Robeson," *Ebony*, February 1951.

148 **"go out of their way to insist"** Essie Robeson, "The Not So Strange Case of Paul Robeson," *California Eagle*, April 5, 1951.

149 **Newcombe had better begin to talk** Essie Robeson, January 29, 1952, Robeson Archives.

149 **"The only thing wrong with Robeson"** *Negro Digest*, March 1950.

149 **At a mammoth Chicago Peace Congress** *Daily Worker*, June 28 and July 2, 1951.

149 **"no other dissenter, whatever his politics"** Ibid.

149 **the famous jazz musician Charlie Parker spotted him** Interview with Chatman Wailes, July 1, 1986.

153 **the diplomatic embarrassment** *Daily Worker,* April 6, 1952.

156 **"I have shouted"** *The Afro-American,* March 13, 1954.

156 **"Is it 'subversive,'"** he asked *Daily Worker,* April 27, 1954.

158 **Robeson hailed the** *Brown v. Board* **decision** *The Afro-American,* December 19, 1953.

Chapter 12: Breakdown and Revival

162 **One recalled the joking remark** Interview with Lee Clayton, April 28, 1982.

163 **He did improve** Multiple conversations with Helen Rosen.

165 **"I'm interested in the place I am in"** Transcript of House Un-American Activities Committee hearing, Robeson Archives.

168 **"They always calm the waters"** Letter from Essie Robeson to George Murphy, Moorland-Spingarn Research Center, Howard University: Murphy.

170 **An FBI report characterized him** FBI New York 100-25857-2927.

172 **he issued a transcendent appeal** Paul Robeson, *Here I Stand* (Beacon Press, 1971), 1–2, 38–40.

173 **There he told the crowd** Tape of the concert at Mother A.M.E. Zion Church, Robeson Archives.

173 **"We keep pinching ourselves"** Letter from Essie Robeson to Glen Byam Shaw, June 30, 1958.

Chapter 13: Broken Health

176 **Old friends who visited felt** Phone interview with Sally Kent Gorton, September 28, 1986.

176 **Raikin had already concluded** Paul Robeson Jr. interview with Bruno Raikin, September 8, 1982.

177 **She decided that it was time** Letter from Essie Robeson to Marilyn and Paul Robeson Jr., January 1959, Robeson Archives.

180 **Essie had been there for the opening** Letter from Essie Robeson to Freda Diamond, April 18, 1959.

183 **become so lonesome** Letter from Paul Robeson to Helen Rosen, November 16, 1959, courtesy Rosen.

184 **"how much he'd aged"** Interview with Andrew Faulds, September 7, 1982.

184 **"a keen desire on his part to get back to America"** Ibid.

184 **"It all gets a little desolate now and then"** Letter from Paul Robeson to Helen Rosen, March 6–7, 1960.

185 **He even expressed the poignant hope** Letter from Paul Robeson to A. Philip Randolph, July 22, 1960, Robeson Archives.

185 **"Maybe you'd better define what you mean"** *National Guardian*, October 1960.

186 **"I'd just knock him down"** *Sydney Morning Herald*, October 13, 1960.

186 **"He is angrier than ever"** Letter from Essie Robeson to Freda Diamond, November 13, 1960, Robeson Archives.

187 **"a wonderful people"** Postcard from Paul Robeson to Clara Rockmore, November 29, 1960, courtesy Rockmore.

187 **he announced he had no further musical ambitions** *New Zealand Woman's Weekly*, November 2, 1960.

188 **"He resents everything I do"** Letter from Essie Robeson to the Rosens, November 26, 1960, courtesy Helen Rosen.

188 **"there is little excuse"** Letters from Lloyd L. Davis to author, January 14 and June 24, 1983.

188 **He felt "terribly, terribly lonely"** Letter from Paul Robeson to Clara Rockmore, December 6, 1960.

189 **to give his courage, knowledge and perception to** Letter from Paul Robeson to the Release of Jomo Kenyatta Committee, January 22, 1961, Robeson Archives.

190 **"and you thank them too for taking me in"** Letters from Paul Robeson to Helen Rosen, February 1961, courtesy Rosen.

191 **"this sort of thing had put him into conflict"** Interview with Dr. Alfred Katzenstein, July 26, 1986.

194 **the result of "nervous exhaustion"** Conversations with Helen Rosen.

196 **"He agreed to that"** Letter from Essie Robeson to the Rosens, February 9, 1962, courtesy Helen Rosen.

199 **"successful fight for a passport"** Letter from John Abt to the Robesons, July 17, 1962, Robeson Archives.

200 **"Thank him for his example and courage"** Letter from Essie Robeson to "Dear Dear Friends," March 17, 1963, Robeson Archives.

201 **"there has been no interruption"** Essie Robeson statement, Robeson Archives.

202 **Dr. Katzenstein found Robeson** Interview with Dr. Alfred Katzenstein, July 26, 1986.

202 **coming to the Buch Clinic** Letter from Essie Robeson to Helen Rosen, October 4 and 15, 1963, courtesy Rosen.

203 **"a tall, gaunt, thin man"** Interview with Kay Pankey, July 26, 1986.

203 **"started to tell anecdotes"** Interview with Ollie Harrington, July 29, 1986.

204 **"He knows you won't expect him to do anything"** Letter from Essie Robeson to family, December 1963, Robeson Archives.

Chapter 14: Falling Silent at Last

205 **"much thinner and not his old vociferous self"** *New York Times*, December 23, 1963.

205 **"His countrymen have proved"** *New York Herald Tribune*, December 25, 1963.

206 **"Paul is so much better"** Letter from Essie Robeson to George Murphy Jr., March 4, 1964, Robeson Archives.

207 **"On a low level, but never mind"** Letter from Essie Robeson to the Rosens, April 10, 1964, courtesy Rosen.

207 **"Like all of you, my heart has been filled"** Paul Robeson, typed statement, August 28, 1964, Robeson Archives.

208 **"to soar like the Eagle"** Paul Robeson, Lorraine Hansberry eulogy, Robeson Archives.

209 **"We too have rejected gradualism and moderation"** Transcript of *Freedomways* salute at Americana Hotel, Robeson Archives.

209 **He expressed, too, his pleasure** Paul Robeson speech at *Freedomways* tribute, Robeson Archives.

210 **"He wants to try things"** Letter from Essie Robeson to family, May 19, 1965, Robeson Archives.

216 **Speaking for the new generation** Letter from Oliver Tambo to June Purdie, December 30, 1967, Robeson Archives.

218 **India's Indira Gandhi recalled** Tributes in Robeson Archives.

222 **They knocked the leaves/From his limbs** Poem from Bil Brown, enclosed in letter to Judge George W. Crockett, November 6, 1977, Robeson Archives.

Image Credits

Page xix: Paul Robeson's 1917–1918 Rutgers yearbook photograph, courtesy of Moorland Spingarn Research Center, Howard University

Page xxi: Paul Robeson in the first-year class at Columbia Law School, 1920, courtesy of Moorland Spingarn Research Center, Howard University

Page 4: The Rex Theatre for Colored People, courtesy of the Library of Congress, Prints and Photographs Division

Page 8: Paul Robeson in his full Rutgers football uniform, courtesy of Paul Robeson Archives, Rutgers University

Page 23: Paul Robeson in the 1925 London production of *The Emperor Jones*, courtesy of Getty Images

Page 26: Paul and Essie Robeson arrive in Manhattan in 1935, courtesy of Getty Images

Page 28: Paul and Paul Jr. in London, courtesy of Moorland Spingarn Research Center, Howard University

Page 30: Paul, Essie, and Paul Robeson Jr., courtesy of the Estate of Carl Van Vechten

Page 36: Paul Robeson and co-star Peggy Ashcroft in *Othello*, courtesy of Moorland Spingarn Research Center, Howard University

Page 44: Paul Robeson and co-star Fredi Washington in *The Emperor Jones* in 1933, courtesy of Alamy Stock Photo

Page 53: Robeson with actress Nina Mae McKinney in *Sanders of the River*, courtesy Alamy Stock Photo

Page 69: Paul Robeson leaves London in 1935 on the first leg of a European tour, courtesy of Getty Images

Page 71: A poster for the film *Song of Freedom*, courtesy of British Lion Films

Page 76: Essie Robeson's mother, known as Ma Goode, and Paul Robeson Jr., courtesy of the Estate of Carl Van Vechten

Page 80: Robeson singing to Loyalist troops in Spain in 1938, courtesy of Moorland Spingarn Research Center, Howard University

Page 98: Paul Robeson and Uta Hagen in *Othello*, courtesy of the Library of Congress

Page 106: Paul Robeson singing at a testimonial dinner in honor of Japanese American World War II, courtesy of Alamy Stock Photo

Page 114: Paul Robeson protesting the Jim Crow segregation policy at Ford's Theater in Baltimore, Maryland, courtesy of Maryland Center for History and Culture

Page 117: Paul Robeson and W.E.B. DuBois at the World Peace Congress in Paris in 1949, courtesy of the Special Collections and University Archives, University of Massachusetts Amherst Libraries

Page 134: Jackie Robinson seen testifying before the House Un-American Activities Committee in 1949, courtesy of AP Images

Page 138: Anti-Robeson demonstration organized by the Joint Veterans Council of Peekskill, courtesy of Granger Historical Picture Archive

Page 146: An issue of the newspaper *Freedom*, jointly founded by Paul Robeson and W.E.B. DuBois, courtesy of Tamiment Library and Robert F. Wagner Labor Archives at New York University

Page 157: Paul Robeson's cancelled U.S. passport, courtesy of South Wales Miners Library

Page 164: Paul Robeson seen testifying before the House Un-American Activities Committee in 1956, courtesy of AP Images

Page 181, Paul Robeson speaking at a London rally in support of nuclear disarmament in 1959, courtesy of Getty Images

Page 182: Paul Robeson with African and Asian students at the World Youth Festival in Vienna, courtesy of Pressefoto Eckebrecht

Page 219: Paul Robeson's obituary in the *New York Amsterdam News* in 1976, courtesy of *New York Amsterdam News*

Page 220: A memorial poster of Paul Robeson, courtesy of the Library of Congress

Index

Note: Page numbers in italics represent photographs and their captions.

About the Author

Martin Duberman is distinguished professor emeritus of history at the CUNY Graduate Center, where he founded and for a decade directed the Center for Lesbian and Gay Studies. The author of more than twenty books—including *Andrea Dworkin, Paul Robeson: A Biography, Radical Acts, Waiting to Land, A Saving Remnant, Howard Zinn, The Martin Duberman Reader,* and *Hold Tight Gently,* all published by The New Press—Duberman has won a Bancroft Prize and been a finalist for both the National Book Award and the Pulitzer Prize. In 2012 Duberman received an honorary doctor of humane letters from Amherst College, and in 2017 an honorary doctor of letters from Columbia University. He lives in New York City.

Publishing in the Public Interest

Thank you for reading this book published by The New Press. The New Press is a nonprofit, public interest publisher. New Press books and authors play a crucial role in sparking conversations about the key political and social issues of our day.

We hope you enjoyed this book and that you will stay in touch with The New Press. Here are a few ways to stay up to date with our books, events, and the issues we cover:

- Sign up at www.thenewpress.com/subscribe to receive updates on New Press authors and issues and to be notified about local events
- Like us on Facebook: www.facebook.com/newpress books
- Follow us on Twitter: www.twitter.com/thenewpress

Please consider buying New Press books for yourself; for friends and family; or to donate to schools, libraries, community centers, prison libraries, and other organizations involved with the issues our authors write about.

The New Press is a 501(c)(3) nonprofit organization. You can also support our work with a tax-deductible gift by visiting www.thenewpress.com/donate.